The
COMPLETE INNKEEPER

Also by Hugh Pitt

The Complete Restaurateur

The
COMPLETE INNKEEPER

The A–Z of Running a Pub

HUGH PITT

ROBERT HALE · LONDON

Photoset in Palatino by
Derek Doyle & Associates, Mold, Clwyd.
Printed in Great Britain by
St Edmundsbury Press, Bury St Edmunds, Suffolk.
and bound by WBC Bookbinders Ltd, Bridgend, Glamorgan.

Contents

for

HAMISH

who made our lives so much easier

Introduction

There are about 103,000 pubs in Britain and it is estimated that at least a quarter of them change hands every year. It would seem to be an industry full of opportunity for the newcomer – especially as eight out of ten of the country's 70,000 free houses are bought by people without any, or very little, previous experience. And therein lies the problem: a very high proportion of those people leave the trade almost as quickly as they came into it. Disappointment, disillusionment, exhaustion, marriage difficulties – all take their toll. A little forethought, a smidgen of experience even serving behind a bar one evening a week, a lot of research and even more careful planning and thinking would have saved an awful lot of heartache and possible financial loss. Which is what this book is all about. It cannot be a substitute for some form of work experience, but it can help you avoid the many and varied pitfalls of the licensed trade. And I hope it will help you enjoy, and succeed in, the challenge of running your own pub.

The title is *The Complete Innkeeper*, but what is the difference between an inn and a pub? To tell the truth the differences have become somewhat blurred, but traditionally an innkeeper was obliged by law to offer shelter and sustenance to travellers, unless he had good reason to refuse them access because of their condition, reputation or because the place was full. Perhaps the first innkeeper most people have ever heard of was the chap (alas unnamed) who had no room for Mary and Joseph when Christ was born. Though I hope you note that he still did the best he could for them – they were not actually left 'out in the cold'. I suppose the story encapsulates all that needs to be said about innkeeping, its duties and traditions. It certainly has a very long history in Britain, the first inns having taken over from the monastic foundations dotted about the country and pledged to help travellers, all of which were abolished by Henry VIII. His daughter, Queen Elizabeth I, spotted, as they say, the resulting gap in the market and decreed that 'New Inns' be established on all major routes a day's ride from each other. Thus we have the curious fact that a great number of places called 'New' are actually among the oldest hostelries in the land.

Of course, as the population became more mobile and the Industrial Revolution concentrated them more and more in cities and sprawling towns, there was no demand for inns in the traditional sense, so the first of the taverns or 'public houses' sprang up. These offered only alcoholic drink to a clientele increasingly thirsty and able to buy relief or even obliteration, if only for an hour or two, from the often awful realities of a long and hard-working day.

In the countryside, though, a more or less static population (few people had ever travelled further than five miles from their birthplace until well towards the end of the nineteenth century) was served refreshment from the back doors of farmhouses, which also made their own cider or brewed their own beer, both drinks coming from their own crops or those of their nearest neighbours. On some of the big estates 'beer houses' were set up specially to serve the workforce, some of whom would have had to walk many miles to get a drink. But it was some years before the 'traditional' convivial inn or pub depicted by Dickens or on Christmas cards came about, if, indeed, it ever existed at all. Hogarth was almost certainly nearer the truth when it came to town taverns which he depicted as nothing more than boozers of the worst kind. It was this sort of place which eventually led to the temperance movement (the evils of the demon drink) and the manipulation of the trade by successive governments, which up to that time had been interested more in ensuring duty was paid on foreign liquor than in those who drank alcohol and in what quantity and where.

The countryman almost certainly fared poorly, with cold, dark, dank hovels, where the now-antique 'settle' was a necessity (albeit a luxurious one) for keeping out the draughts in front of an evilly smoking ingle-nook fireplace in a 'house' selling cloudy, musty-tasting beer or muddy cider, where any stranger could be certain of indifference, hostility or even worse. Some may think that the situation is little better today in some so-called 'hostelries'. Which is yet another reason why I hope this book will help the aspiring licensee.

1 Having What It Takes

The 'Number One' Priority

In any list of questions about how to find a pub, how to raise the money, how to get experience and so on, the most essential and important priority in the order of thinking is quite often overlooked – you. Yes, you. The putative landlord or landlady is the one factor which is going to make or break your new business, or have your new business make or break you. And here can I make a plea for understanding: I am going to use the term landlord rather than constantly referring to the landlord or landlady which becomes rather tiresome. By landlord I mean everyone who keeps an inn or pub.

Now you do not need the keenest observation to realize that some landlords should never really have contemplated taking a pub. One often asks, why did they do it? They are unwelcoming, taciturn and surly. Or they are chatterboxes who can never mind their own business and persist in telling their customers all their own woes. On the whole, but by no means exclusively, they are the owners of free houses who have bought their way into the trade, or tenants of pubs which belong to a smaller brewery whose tenancy selection is not all that it should be. The larger breweries, whatever their faults, are nowadays very keen on tenant selection procedures, as we shall see in Chapter 3, and do try to suit the right people to the right house.

Now neither of the above examples of landlord would in normal circumstances last very long, as a dwindling supply of customers would mean increasingly diminishing returns. Indeed, in your search for the sort of pub you want you may well come across just such a place – on the way down or at rock bottom. Keep an eye open for it; you may get a bargain.

The Physical and Mental Demands

But back to you. In the first place you must have good health. Running a pub is extremely demanding physically, there is quite a lot of heavy shifting work, especially in the cellar department, and stacking or 'bottling up' in the bar areas. Gas cylinders are heavy too, and although good cellar design, as we shall see, goes a long way to taking the old-fashioned back-break out of the work of shifting barrels on and off their stillages there are times when a bit of solid muscle is needed.

Now that is not to say that you have to be built like Charles Atlas, just that you must be fit and able to take the punishment of long working hours and hard physical labour. But there is another consideration too. Your new life will be very taxing mentally. You must never underestimate this: mental exhaustion is every bit as dangerous as physical.

Now it is said that anyone who wants any type of pub must be barmy to start with, or if not, at least half-way to being short of a few bricks to a full hod. Be that as it may, your own character will shape what the pub is to become. You must have a disposition which is cheerful, outgoing, friendly, understanding and gregarious, with a capacity to listen to other people's problems and opinions without necessarily airing your own. At the same time, you must be capable of clear-headed thinking, with an acute understanding of business as well as human character.

Now I shall stress continually the need for some form of 'hands on' work experience, however humble, before applying for, or buying, a public house. Just one evening behind a busy bar will show you more of the realities than any textbook, innkeeping course or chat with a friendly landlord from the other side of the bar where you are sitting on a stool as a customer. And if you can augment bar work on a Saturday evening, say, by clearing up late that night and then cleaning and bottling up early the next morning, then I guarantee you really will wonder about becoming a landlord yourself, ready to open again at midday and still have enough energy to laugh rather than cry. Contrary to the cosy opinions of most customers, keeping a pub is not just a matter of pulling a few pints while indulging in pleasant conversation with the regulars. Keeping a pub is being a professional in a very difficult and demanding job. It is your profession to encourage customers to come into your pub and not someone else's; to see that those customers are properly treated and made to feel at home; and to run the business properly, make a decent profit and ensure a decent future for yourself.

In the mean time it is as well to bear in mind that one of the most important attributes of a good publican is an optimistic cheerfulness; the licensed trade can be a lot of fun. Indeed, on the list of attributes already demanded of you it would be very odd if you were not determined to enjoy such an intriguing adventure. You will be working for yourself and what you put into that work will see a definite return, not always immediately but certainly in time. It is almost like building your own house, brick by brick, until it is exactly how you wished it to be. Even then it will not be finished, there will constant extra touches to be added, improvements and polish. I know there will also be a few heartbreaks, a great many periods of depression, times when you say to yourself, 'Why the hell am I stuck in this ...?' Believe me, I know what it is like. And so does every other landlord or landlady throughout the trade, throughout the country. Which is perhaps why they all tend to huddle together, if huddle is not too strong a word, because they know what life can chuck at them.

2 *Which Pub?*

Planning The Pub You Want
So, where do you start? How do you start? Well, the first thing you do *not* do is rush out to your nearest estate agent, put your own house on the market and then tear around the agents which specialize in selling inns or pubs, or start approaching brewers to see if they have any vacancies for tenants or managers. No. You do quite a lot of thinking. And the first thing you think about is what sort of pub you have in mind. Sit down and write out *exactly* what you have in mind, *exactly* the sort of place you reckon you can run happily and successfully.

For instance: what size of pub do you want? Do you want a pub in a large town-centre or on, say, a housing estate? Do you want a pub somewhere in a large city, or in a small country town or even a village? With one or two possible exceptions your own choice will be the same as hundreds of others anxious to get into the trade – and some of those people will have thought in great detail, so you must do the same.

The Locale of Your Local: Town vs. Country
Next think about where, what part of the country. Just because you live in Bacup does not mean that Bodmin will be similar. In fact there may well be a case for staying within the general area you know well. You will know what the local people are like, what their preferences and habits are, even how they like their pubs and what sort of beer they drink. Remember, unlike restaurants and similar outlets where very detailed research is needed before starting up a new one, or even taking over one already in existence, most pubs are sited for very good and

traditional reasons. Many have been there for a great many years, some even centuries. Comparatively few are 'new' in the sense that they were purpose-built to serve a very definite catchment area, be it industrial, administrative, residential or a shopping centre. But in some cases, the traditional reasons for pubs being in one particular place have long since disappeared even though the pub remains standing, so some detailed research will be needed. In many industrial areas whole blocks have been bulldozed and the local workforce moved away to cleaner, more congenial surroundings, leaving the public house forlornly trying to serve a clientele which no longer exists. These places are the exceptions I mentioned above. Few people want them unless there is some gleam of renewal of the whole area, in which case they can become very valuable. But until that does happen, they will need a lot of capital set aside just to keep going until any form of profit appears. Hardly the place, one would think, for any newcomer, however cheap the asking price. Such places are best left to the 'big boys' unless you are a very clever businessman.

In the countryside, some villages have become stagnant, their population having dwindled to nothing, the old village pub serving no one and no purpose. In a great many English villages, sometimes quite small, there were sometimes two or three 'locals' (nothing more than ale houses in reality) where none now exists, because of what the experts call the 'demographic shift' (that is, no one lives there any more). There are an increasing number of moribund pubs in the British countryside. Take no notice of whatever the big breweries say in their advertisements about their keeping the English country pub alive and thriving. It is all a cynical exercise in public relations. The big breweries are the first to close or sell off any pub which does not give sufficient return on their investment, and the poor licensee (as we shall see, often on only a year's tenancy agreement) is of no account at all in the boardroom. Even so, the breweries do on occasion get their fingers burned through lack of research, spending large sums of money on new 'themes', ludicrous gimmicks like 'welcome parlours', only to find that new by-passes are to be built, new or improved roads have taken passing trade away to another more convenient route or new breathalyser laws have hit what was traditionally a motorists' watering-hole. It should also be said that many breweries have sold off inns and pubs which they considered to have too hopeless a future, or which were too unprofitable for their own needs, only to have them transformed into cheerful, money-spinning establishments by some young couple who had the get-up-and-go to see their real potential as free houses, uncluttered by restrictive clauses imposed by a distant brewery.

But remember too that it is not only the big cities which have changed, so have the smaller country towns. And go on changing all the time. Thirty years ago my local country town with a population of 16,000 had forty-one licensed houses, some competing literally side by side. It now has fourteen – still too many, perhaps, but to an outsider (and certainly to publicans themselves) there is a deep and curious mystery about why some pubs are popular and others not, independent from considerations of their position. There is no simple reason why some pubs can still exist, and do good business, even though they have apparent competition virtually next door. These are among the puzzling factors that any newcomer must consider. I know of some country pubs, well run, in an 'obviously' good position, which seem never to get off the ground, while others, often difficult or well-nigh impossible to find are packed full. It is the same with most towns. Why do men and women walk past four pubs, say, in the same street to have a glass of something in a fifth which quite often is down an alleyway and apparently has nothing going for it at all? Ah … there you have it. What are pubs for? And what is special about the one you have in mind, or would like to run? Why should people come to you and not to the one next door? If you believe it is merely a matter of whether you have or do not have music, one-armed bandits, pool tables, a dartboard, good and swift service, even palatable food then you are going to be desperately disappointed. Because it is something quite indefinable – even among pubs belonging to the same brewery and selling the same drinks at the same prices.

I think it worth while to consider this a little more before continuing. It is true that certain pubs, mainly in big city-centres, will do a roaring trade, especially at lunchtime, simply because they are the nearest to blocks of offices and there is little point in walking further than you need if you do not have much time. Most such places, you would think, are natural money-spinners. But this is not always true, largely because they are full only for about two hours a day and in the evening practically deserted, as are the streets around them. Now you cannot make a tremendous financial success on about two hours a day, five days a week. Rent, rates, heating, lighting and perhaps staff cost money all day, all week, mornings and evenings. There is also a famous phrase in the trade to the effect that 'packed pubs don't make money'. It means that when a pub gets too popular, too full, people go somewhere else because 'you can never get to the bar at so-and-so's'. Thus the trade eventually dwindles and the poor landlord very often wonders why. But, on the other hand, do not be misled by how *apparent* the 'busyness' is of any house. Do not fall into the trap of ordinary customers who believe that 'their' pub is always busy and cheerful just because it so happens to be when they normally go there for a pint. As a potential landlord you must keep an eye on the sort of place you want to run morning and evening, weekends too, high-days and holidays. Alas, the trade is full of pitfalls for the unwary (and for the very wary indeed) and no one has the exact answers.

In addition are some types of pubs, very often technically inns with accommodation, which are sited in most curious places and which appeal to putative landlords because of their very remoteness. Not all of these, by any means, are free houses, since the breweries often hold on to such properties as they can see much greater potential in the long-term than they apparently offer now.

Take an example: it was always the custom for British canals to have pubs sited at strategic intervals along their banks. These houses were quite often a long way from any major centre or catchment area and frequently a long way from any decent road. They were there simply to serve a working, boating, passing trade. And as the canals began to lose their importance so too did the canal-side pubs. Most simply gave up. A few had the good fortune to be sufficiently picturesque and reachable by a newly mobile population, which sustained them or even dramatically increased their trade. Then came the leisure revolution. Quite suddenly canals became good news. In the case of at least one, the Kennet & Avon, which runs through the middle of southern England, a host of volunteers over a period of about ten years restored virtually the entire system, bringing with it new boats, marinas, people. One or two brewers which had not got rid of their canal-side pubs suddenly realized the potential and began to upgrade them all, whether successfully or not I have no idea. They doubtless now wish they owned more.

Similarly some pubs exist for other specific reasons. Walkers, especially in mountainous areas or regions of natural beauty, are bringing a new lease of life to many pubs, hitherto moribund. And in many cases accommodation is the key to greater success, something we shall consider in a later chapter. The same is true of pubs serving other sectors: anglers, fly-fishermen, even hang-gliders and hot-air ballooners. It is all part of the leisure boom – the fact that people have more time and more money to spend than in the days when many of these old pubs served a very different customer, like bargees, cattle-drovers, shepherds, navvies and tinkers.

But in case this all sounds a little idyllic, I would urge you to think very carefully before rural fever attacks you. Go back to earlier in this chapter. Decide what sort of pub would suit you. Do not be side-tracked by visions of cosy, olde-worlde pubs in remote and apparently glamorous areas. On the other hand bear in mind what many of the recruiting managers of the big breweries say: it is the *quality* of life which is now attracting more and more applicants to the licensed trade. Given two pubs of similar size and money-earning potential, but one in the country and one in the town, the country pub will have five people after it for every one wanting the town site. This was not true many years ago.

On the other hand I would warn you very seriously that life in the country is quite different to what people who have spent all their lives in cities believe. Beware the 'green wellie' syndrome: a holiday in a country cottage or the odd weekend with friends is quite different to the countryside in, say, winter where in some areas men trample mud through your bars, or come in stinking of silage if only for a packet of cigarette papers and a palmful of Golden Virginia. Once again, stick to what you know about, the area you feel confident about or at home in, at least for your first venture into the pub trade. You will have more than enough worries just learning to run a pub without burdening yourself with even more, such as the suspicions of country people, their apparently unwelcoming manner, their resentment of change. Such attitudes are not all one-way. Someone from the country who takes a pub in a town or large conurbation may feel at odds with the townies' lack of courtesy, uncaring attitudes, rushing lifestyle and off-hand behaviour.

Beer and Atmosphere
Finally, however, there are one or two key points to bear in mind. They may seem obvious once you have read them but they are by no means as apparent as they should be to incomers.

Beer. People still go to pubs for a glass of beer. It might sometimes seem as though they are there for crisps, wine, spirits, pool table, darts and so on but you would be wrong. Beer, good beer, is still the first and foremost reason why the vast mass of money-spending drinkers go into a pub. Now it matters not whether you drink beer or your wife only drinks gin. Beer is still first and foremost the reason men go into pubs and womenfolk follow.

Atmosphere. With the exception of huge, city-centre 'boozers', people go to a pub because they like the atmosphere, the conviviality and the feeling that a drink gives them of being a cross between Oscar Wilde and Socrates. There is nothing extraordinary about this, whatever the anti-drink lobby says in its superior fashion.

Alcohol is a great lubricant for the tongue, the conscience, the ambition, the sexual urge, a great source of innocent happiness and harmless bonhomie and has always been thus. People who abuse alcohol have only themselves to blame, despite the modern and idiotic fashion of putting all the blame on the man or woman who serves the drink or the organization which manufactures it. These latter-day attitudes are designed carefully to shift blame and responsibility on to shoulders more easily targeted, as it is now unfashionable to castigate a man who cannot 'hold his drink' – behaviour considered a social crime in my young days. Drink is also, of course, a great way to get people talking, to become part of a group, to 'join in'. But it also allows some people to be comfortably alone. This may surprise you, but any observant landlord will tell you the same. I was always touched by some of the regular customers we had in our inn. They would come in at least once a week, on their own, and have one or two drinks without even trying to talk to anyone else, including my wife and me. We often wondered who they were, where they came from, why they came to us and no one else, whether they were painfully shy. They were certainly not antisocial in so far as they were polite, neat and seemed perfectly normal in every other way. It was just that they sat entirely on their own and showed no inclination to talk to anyone about anything. But there were lessons to be learned from their behaviour: in the first place it was none of our business who they were or why they were there if they did not wish to tell us; and in the second place the very fact that they were there, and regularly, meant that we appealed to them in some way. In other words, without quite knowing why, we were doing a good job and these people felt at home in our place and not in someone else's. That was not a bad endorsement, you might think, of our attitudes and policy. But before such smugness becomes insufferable, one has to admit that for every person who liked the way we did things, I bet you we could find two people who hated it. And that is one of the problems: I firmly believe that you cannot, and should not try to be everything to all people all the time. I honestly believe that even if such an aim were possible to achieve such a pub would turn out to be such a bland compromise that it would put people off rather than attract them in. Now I know that many people, especially brewery chairmen, would dispute such a statement, because they endeavour to maintain the fiction that all pubs, their pubs anyway, are equally good, well run, 'customer-sympathetic'. This attitude has led, distressingly I think, to the awful sameness of the British public house, so much so that it is often difficult to tell what part of the country one is in, because the decor, furnishings, lay-out and above all choice of food have all stemmed from the same cramped attitudes of mind.

As a landlord you may well have to toe some brewery line if you are a tenant or manager, but never forget that you must be your own man or woman even though you need the attributes we discussed in Chapter 1. That is what brings people in and makes money.

The public house is not just a business owned by a brewery, one link in a chain of licensed retail outlets owned by some amorphous, mindless conglomerate, however the directors of such an outfit would like to regard 'their' pubs. No: it is what the landlord and landlady make it. People – customers – come to one pub or another not to satisfy the balance sheet of some grey company secretary or accountant. They come because of you. And I shall continue to stress this point continually throughout the book.

3   Weighing Up the Options

The 'Big Six'
The licensed trade in Britain is dominated by six huge
brewery chains: Bass, Grand Metropolitan, Allied Breweries, Whitbread, Courage and Scottish & Newcastle, who
together own almost 34,000 pubs. Though this represents
only a third of the total, nevertheless the 'big six' account
for three-quarters of all beer sales – a massive turnover of
£9 billion a year.

Attempts by politicians to upset what is a near
monopoly have always come to naught. The breweries are
well organized, massively financed and manipulate a
number of MPs as a powerful and effective lobby in
Parliament.

These 'big boys' – with the possible exception of Grand
Metropolitan which we shall consider later – are obviously
the model for the way the whole industry is run. Even if
you do not apply directly to one of them for a
managership or a tenancy you will not be able to avoid
dealing with them at some stage in your new career, if
only to buy some of their branded lines, which are heavily
promoted throughout the country and without which no
pub would be complete.

Apart from these six, there are a number of smaller,
independent breweries some of which own their own
pubs, from two or three to a hundred or more while others,
often in out-of-the-way rural areas, sell to any landlord
who takes 'guest beers', as they are now termed. The way
pubs are made available is, however, much the same
throughout the country, although recruitment methods
(called 'personnel selection') is now a highly refined art
among the larger groups. This, in turn, has resulted in

fewer failures, by which I mean landlords proving unsuitable, unprofitable or dissatisfied in some way. Smaller breweries may offer tenancies on a rather more hit-and-miss, less scientific system, but for the most part they are none the worse for that. Indeed, to many first-timers looking for a pub they may well be more attractive, as they do not have that insistence on regimentation and 'corporate image' so beloved of the huge conglomerates.

The Tied House
Anyway, let us first take a look at the tied house system.

A tied house is the term for a pub which is 'tied' to, i.e. owned by, a brewery. The tenant, who is the man or woman who actually holds the justices' licence to sell liquor, has to agree to all sorts of conditions and rules laid down by the brewery, not only as regards his opening hours but what beer he can sell and so on. The rigidity of some of these rules has been relaxed recently, for example 'guest' beers (that is, beer brewed by a brewer outside the conglomerate) can be sold, and not all spirits, wines and soft drinks have to be bought from the main brewery as used to be the case. But do not get the idea that the relaxation of some of the rules (largely as a result of political pressure) has meant a new freedom for tenants. Breweries are not run nowadays as they used to be, that is by brewers – men skilled in the making of beer and anxious to promote its values and properties to more and more drinkers. No, breweries are run by accountants with smart legal eagles at their sides, both of whom are adept at moving the goalposts when under threat. A tenant is, in reality, 'tied' hand, foot and finger to that brewery and increasingly leases are written only for twelve months, as opposed to terms of years sometime ago. There is very little security of tenure, and rent 'reviews', as well as a simple non-renewal of a lease, can be used to shift tenants who have irritated the brewery, or who do not show enough return by way of profit. None of the big breweries will admit publicly why leases are now on an annual basis, but you may bet your bottom dollar that it is advantageous to the brewery to have them thus and the tenant has hardly been considered.

Rents for tied houses are assessed in terms of 'barrelage' – that is, the number of barrels of beer you sell (or are expected to sell) every year. Other drinks like bottled beers, spirits, even 'mixers' like tonic water, bitter lemon and so on also contribute towards this barrelage providing they are all bought from the brewery. As an example, twelve crates of mixers and a case of whisky may count as a barrel of beer but the commuted figure will be discussed and explained by the brewery at your interview. There is no set quantity in the trade for barrelage equivalents. Each brewery lays down its own rules, but bear in mind that barrelage is also used as a basis for brewers' loans, which may be offered for improvements to both their tied-house tenants and to the landlords of free houses.

Not unnaturally it is a source of irritation to many tenants that their own hard work and increasing liquor sales are all too often seen by their landlords as a chance to increase the rents dramatically each year. This can be particularly galling given that the products bought (by legal agreement) from the landlord brewery actually cost the tenant more than they would do in the open market. Yes, I am afraid so; the tenant of a tied house has to pay more for a barrel of beer (or bottle of whisky) bought from his landlord than the owner of a free house or corner shop does. The brewery has got the tenant every which way, make no mistake.

The Tenancy Selection Procedure

Now so far this has been all rather negative, a bit 'anti' brewery. But there are some very definite pros to set against the cons of being a tied-house tenant. Let us take a look at this side of the coin.

In the first place it is very often the only way ordinary people without vast sums of capital behind them can get into the trade at all. It obviously costs very much less to become a tenant than it will to buy your own free house. To this end a careful selection procedure is followed, calculated to fit the right applicant to the right tenancy. The process starts with a form to be filled in which will be sent to you by the tied house manager, or the recruitment division if the brewery is a large one.

This form will often be quite lengthy, asking you to provide such details as your full names, number and ages of children or other dependants, education, previous employment record, experience in the licensed trade or a similar job such as catering, marketing and so on, your financial standing and the name of your bank, what part of the country you prefer and whether you have ever been convicted by a court for any offence, even a minor one to do with traffic. Remember that in this connection the police have to report to the licensing justices on the suitability or otherwise of anyone applying to hold a liquor licence. You may also be asked to enclose recent photographs.

Along with this form will come an attractively produced brochure detailing the benefits of holding a tenancy with that particular brewery. It will be illustrated with typical pubs within the group and pictures of happy licensees and their spouses, and will detail a range of products you will be able to offer to a public only too eager to buy them from you in vast (and profitable) quantity.

In most cases invitations to apply for tenancies stipulate a husband and wife team or 'partners' of some sort, with the implication that such a partnership should have a provenly stable history, whether between unmarried couples or friends of the same sex. It is possible for a single man or woman to take on a tenancy. The pub itself, however, would have to lend itself to such an arrangement as regards position, size and so on. A person on his or her own would also have to offer very special and desirable qualities, with considerable work experience in the trade, to make any brewery take even a second glance at such an application. Years ago, of course, a landlord's wife would have been of no importance in the selection of a tenant, but what many breweries insist on calling a 'family atmosphere' is now deemed to be achievable only by a husband and wife team, albeit without small children. There is probably a greater chance for single men and women in city centre pubs of no great character – places for which tenants are now becoming increasingly difficult to find.

If your answers to the first questionnaire are satisfactory

you will be asked to attend at least one in-depth interview, which will include questions designed to test your determination to succeed, knowledge of the trade and your own ideas as to the sort of pub you want and how you would want to run it, as well as that all-important question – how much of your own money are you prepared to put into the business?

If you are then thought suitable in principle you will be expected to go on an initial 'induction' training course, which will last for up to five days. It is designed to cover every aspect not only of running a pub generally, but of running that brewery's pub. It will include licensing and commercial law, cellar management, cash flow, book-keeping, profit and loss accounts, stock-taking, hygiene, bar operation, marketing, budgeting and general financial control, as well as brewery visits (sessions designed to give aspirants a good grounding in 'product knowledge'), and ending up with the pulling of a 'perfect pint'. It will cost about £500, plus dinner, bed and breakfast but the 'package' very often makes provision for free day courses in the future on specialized topics which will also include (useful this), training sessions for any staff you may recruit. (It is true that similar courses are run by brokers and agents in the trade, of variable worth, it must be admitted, but as we shall see in the free-house section, many lending institutions now insist new landlords go on such courses as a condition of getting a loan.)

These courses are by no means easy and a 'pass' at the end will be necessary before any pub is offered to the applicants. Tactfully, those in charge of these training courses only tell their class whether they have passed if *all* have made the grade. If some have failed everyone is told their results will be notified to them in the post.

An interesting sideline of some of these courses is a section on your own well-being and good intentions, particularly that of drinking. It has to be said, sadly, that alcoholism among publicans ranks just ahead of that among doctors, and all landlords are well advised to watch this aspect very carefully. One of the big breweries asks everyone who takes their landlord courses to write down, and seal into an envelope, their 'good intentions' regarding personal drinking, time off and so on. The new tenants then put their own names and the address of their new pub on to the envelope. This is left with the head of recruitment, kept for three months, and then posted (still sealed) on to the new tenant. The effect, I am assured, is often said to be quite shattering. I can well believe it. But the fact that you have acquitted yourself well in the initial interviews and have then passed the training course does not mean you are home and dry.

At some later stage you will be asked to look at a pub – one that the brewery thinks may be suitable for you. But success in getting it will be based on your carrying out a very carefully researched, written 'presentation' about the property, detailing why it appeals to you, what potential it has from your point of view and how you intend to develop, expand or improve its business potential. In other words, how will you run the place compared to the present, outgoing tenant, so that you get a decent living and the brewery a decent profit? It will be on that document that your chances depend. So make sure you have done your homework.

So, you have passed everything with flying colours. What next? Well, you will probably be offered that pub – at a price.

The Inntrepreneur System

Now I mentioned earlier in this chapter that Grand Metropolitan is the exception to the general tied-house situation in Britain. Perhaps because of the dangers of political and public pressures on the huge conglomerates, or because in all honesty they think it best for their trade and the properties they own, Grandmet some time back pioneered their Inntrepreneur scheme, by which the traditional tenant and landlord system was replaced by a 'licensed retailer' deal. Grandmet's houses are offered on a straight, full repairing twenty-year lease to suitable applicants. In effect the new lessee buys part of the equity (a 'slice of the action'), and is no longer simply a tenant to be held on an annual tenancy agreement.

Because of the head-in-the-sand attitudes of the licensed trade generally, and in particular the traditional resentment of the Licensed Victuallers Association to anything new, this move by Grandmet was viewed with the deepest suspicion and mistrust, even though it was no different to the system by which many free houses throughout Britain change hands anyway, the freehold not being owned by a brewery but by a private owner, perhaps a family or a trust of some sort.

The Grandmet scheme proved instantly popular and within the first eighteen months about 1,800 licensed premises had been leased under this new system. By the end of 1990 a total of 3,500 pubs was the target. Altogether there were 60,000 applicants for Grandmet pubs and by the beginning of 1990 a total of 2,500 'suitable candidates' were on the waiting list.

The ingoings expected from the new lessees were between £30,000 and £50,000 – in effect, it is fair to point out, not very much greater than for normal tied houses and certainly cheaper than the average free house. There is, of course, one basic difference between being a tenant in a tied house and a lessee of Inntrepreneur.

As we have already seen, tied-house tenants for the most part have only annual leases nowadays. The Inntrepreneur leases are for twenty years, with a rent review every five years – a review, Grandmet insists, which will take no account of improvements to the property the lessee has made at his own expense – and they are completely assignable at any time, which means you can sell the lease to another person if you so wish, along with the normal contents, furniture and fittings and stock in hand which you own anyway. A further difference is the supply agreement by which only beer and cider has to be bought from Grandmet companies; other drinks and all other supplies can be bought from whoever you wish.

Under the Inntrepreneur system the future of the pub is very much your own future. The harder you work, the more likely it is to improve not only as a business but as a future investment. What is in effect an asset you have bought will go on gaining value just as your own house might do, except that in this case (and unlike the tradition of the tied house) the goodwill is also assessable (and therefore of value to you) just like any normal business sale.

'Managed' Pubs

Of course, you may not have sufficient money for the ingoing costs of even a small public house, tied or not, yet still be passionate about a career in the trade. In that case there is no need to despair, since a great many pubs are not only tied but what is called 'managed'. Breweries decide not to let pubs on a tenancy basis for a number of greatly varied reasons. In some cases, particularly with very busy city pubs, the brewery reckons it can make a lot more money for itself by putting in a manager and paying him or her a straight salary like any other employee. Such a person will almost certainly have had some hands-on experience in the trade but even so there will be a probationary period after a training course. In larger pubs there will be assistant manager jobs available and with some breweries relief managers are employed to take over when other staff have days off or holidays.

This sort of entry to the trade is an excellent introduction and will put you in a good position for a tenancy of your own with either your present employers or another brewery. Moreover, borrowing money to acquire a free house will be less of a problem because you will be deemed less of a risk. Many breweries are only too pleased to help their own people get on once they have the necessary experience and are found to be honest, diligent and enterprising. But such jobs are not a get-rich-quick opportunity and woe betide you if you are ever caught with your hand in the till as, alas, so many managers are. You will never get a job in the licensed business again. For all its apparent size the trade, free and tied, operates the fastest early-warning network known to science and you will have a bad reputation before even you yourself know about it.

As we have seen, getting a tenancy is not always an easy task and hands-on experience is essential but if you don't really mind where you work while actually getting such experience then bear in mind that pubs in big cities or towns are often more easily available than ones in, say, suburban or rural areas. It all boils down to the quality of life and recruitment managers from the big breweries have admitted to me that this is of increasing importance nowadays in attracting the right sort of tenant. The 'roses round the door' idyll is still alive and well and living in the heart of most would-be licensees. In fact, on a visit to London not so long ago I saw an advertisement in an Underground train for trainee management couples for a well-known brewery. If breweries have to use that sort of advertising to get licensees, I thought, things must have come to a pretty pass. Indeed they have, in some city areas, but it cannot be knocked as a valuable introduction to the whole licensed trade.

Be careful about some management jobs, however. They are often not quite what they seem, the term 'manager' often having been cheapened to mean a job no better than that of a servile errand boy. This is not so with the more reputable breweries, to be fair, but it is particularly applicable to free-house owners anxious to get staff on the cheap. For all their glib advertising and gushy promises at interview, always insist on seeing the sort of accommodation offered. You will often be in for an unpleasant surprise but do not believe any blandishments that the builders are about to come in and do the place up, or a promise that it will 'all be different by the time you come'. You have my solemn guarantee that it will be no such thing. Leave the place at once: yes, you need experience, but not that sort, for in reality you will learn very little about the actual business of running a pub, just the fetching and carrying chores which you could learn in any other job but probably get better paid for it.

Acquiring a Free House
So far, in this chapter, we have considered working for someone else, apart from the Inntrepreneur scheme, which is the closest you can get to working for yourself within a brewery's ambit. But a free house is still the ambition of a great many people, whether they know anything about the trade or not. Indeed, nearly eight out

of ten free houses in Britain are bought by people without any experience of the licensed trade whatsoever.

Obviously a free house is going to cost you a lot more than a tenancy as you will be buying the whole place, lock, stock and barrel. But whatever the size of your wallet do take care to buy a house within your needs, abilities and ambitions. So first you must think about the complexities and problems such a business will bring – a business in which you will stand or fall entirely by your own decisions.

However, you are not silly. You have done as I suggested and written down exactly the sort of place you want and we shall consider in the next chapter how you set about finding such a place.

Of course, if you have owned an ordinary dwelling house you will be familiar with all the basic things which also apply to a pub: mortgages, insurance and so on. Obviously there are rather more problems than just those, not the least of which will be that you have to pay not only increased insurances but your poll tax or community charge, plus a hefty whack of extra money in the form of the uniform business rate – because you are a dwelling *and* a business property you become eligible for both. These figures may be quite high, and you would do well to bear them in mind in all the sums you are going to have to do. But those are not the only differences. For example, although you will, certainly, have your own dwelling, and all your own furniture and so on about you, the very fact that you are living in a business means that it must come first. From the very outset you will discover just how little time you are going to have to 'get straight', to attend to even the most ordinary needs, chores, routines of your previous life. The number of hours in any day will suddenly appear to be quite inadequate. Sheer exhaustion may well tempt you to abandon all practical measures to 'begin as you mean to go on'. But this is an essential ingredient of your future success. Earlier I told you to write down all sorts of things, including how you intended to run your pub. Stick by them, and stick to your determination to have a day off.

First of all, however, forget what all sorts of people will

tell you about the licensed trade, about the law forcing you to be open all the time within the permitted hours, about not closing for a day off or not closing on take-over day, (which is depressing enough as it is without having to stay open), as the somewhat greedy breweries insist their tenants do.

In a free house you are your own man. Providing you stay within the law of 'permitted hours' you can do as you please, theoretically never opening at all – although such a course of action would allow magistrates to revoke your liquor licence upon the application of members of the public, the police or other licensees. You could hardly be considered a 'fit and proper person' to hold a licence if you never actually opened your doors to anyone wanting to buy liquor. But from the start, you do have enormous freedom. But this confers enormous responsibility too. Being your own man could also cause you to drift up the creek without the paddle of guidance you would otherwise get from your brewery if you were a tenant. So who is going to hold your hand?

Well, before dealing with that I want to stress once again that you go on a course of innkeeping. As I mentioned before, some are better than others, but the brokers through whom you bought your free house will probably be able to suggest suitable courses, as will the Licensed Victuallers Association, either locally or nationally in London. Expect to pay about £500 per person, or about £850 per couple. They are often held in hotels in various towns throughout Britain, last for three or four days and the fee you pay will include accommodation and meals.

First to call will probably be the brewery reps whose beer has traditionally been sold by the pub you have just bought. Competition is pretty fierce throughout the trade but do not sign any agreements or make too many promises. Just listen to what they all have to say, make notes if necessary, and suggest a time for them to see you again. I shall cover this whole question of reps later in the book but at this stage I just want to reassure you that help is actually much nearer than you think; men and women of considerable knowledge are there to share their advice, experience and wisdom with you. Latch on to them. As a brief example, my wife and I took over a very run-down pub and even we were astonished to see how low some of the prices were, but we felt it wrong to alter them too quickly. The day after we opened a rep from one of the big soft drinks and 'mixers' companies called to see us. He looked round the shelves of the bar, turned to us and said quite pleasantly: 'Are you going to shut up shop now, or give it another day or two? At these prices it would be simpler to give my stuff away!'

He spent the next two hours repricing every single item on the shelves. And remember, he repriced in line not only with his company's recommendations, but with what other pubs were charging locally and with the sort of pub we had just taken over. 'Later,' he told us, looking round the seedy, grubby bar, 'you can charge more but not until you've smartened the place up a bit.' That man became a firm mentor and friend and has remained so ever since.

Marriages, Families and Partnerships

So *you* are OK, fit, cheerful, raring to go. But what about the family? If you are married, is your spouse quite as keen on the idea as you are? Just bear in mind that it is virtually impossible, for one or the other of a married couple to continue following their own (different) career, job and interests. It is highly unlikely any brewery would offer you a tied house or a management deal unless both partners were fully committed, and I would pretty much guarantee that disaster lurks round the corner for anyone contemplating buying a free house with such an arrangement in mind. The problem is, keeping a pub is a full-time occupation which sucks in whole families, certainly a wife or husband, however initially unwilling one of them might have been. It is depressing to have to say this but the licensed trade, like the catering trade, plays havoc with marriages, so if you are married you must hope that the union has a strong foundation and that each of you is as keen on being an innkeeper or publican as the other.

But while on the subject of marriages a word on partnerships. Although, as we shall see, it may be better for legal reasons to have a partnership agreement between a husband and wife running a pub, it is a sure-fire recipe for calamity if you enter into any partnership with, say, another couple, or one or two friends. There are natural temptations about partnerships. Working with someone else often means you will have more capital for a bigger or better pub or perhaps two skills can be employed – one running the bar, if that is one partner's interest, and the other running the kitchen, if that partner has been a chef or in the catering trade. Listen to none of these 'reasons'. Be tempted by no argument in their favour. A very experienced representative of one of the big breweries once told me that partnerships of that sort always fall apart. It is merely a matter of time. Some might last for years, but fall apart they eventually will. It is a fact of the trade and I shall mention it again later.

So, you have a good marriage – but what about the children? I am not entirely persuaded that a pub is 'no place to bring up a family', as is often said. I know many pubs where families seem to be happy and fulfilled but I do think it hard on children to be left alone for too long when young, simply because mother and father have to work and there is no place for them on either side of the bar, whether because of often stupid licensing laws or just because they would 'get in the way'. It should be a matter left to your discretion – it depends on what sort of parents you are and on the sort of place you want. I am sure some pubs would be ideal for children, especially when they are in the country or with decent living accommodation and big enough for a staff which would allow at least one of the couple regular and adequate amounts of time off with the kids. I am not a marriage guidance counsellor and how you bring up your own children must be your concern, but do bear them in mind when considering a pub and carefully weigh up all the pros and cons. If in any doubt, wait until they are grown up.

Now all the things I have mentioned – your own character and outlook, the attitudes of your spouse, the situation *vis-á-vis* children – will in turn dictate to a great extent the type of house you will be after when you decide to take the final plunge.

4 Finance

Research

Having explained as much as I can about the way breweries and pubs are organized in Britain you still have to find one of your own. So how do you set about it?

Well, in Chapter 2 I mentioned that you had to decide on a particular area, in general terms. Having done that you must do a lot of research in that area to find out which brewery owns what pubs, if you want a tied house, and just how many free houses there may be. Incidentally, detailed research is never wasted – some areas of Scotland are actually 'dry' – that is, they have no pubs, licensed hotels or off-licences within their boundaries.

The 'Carve-Up'

But wherever you decide to settle it is no good carrying out detailed research at long distances – and no research is worth while unless it is very detailed indeed. You just have to get down there and spend some time touring round. Note, in the first instance, the numbers of pubs which are owned by one of the big conglomerates which I named in Chapter 3. And by the word 'note' I mean note – write every single thing down in a workbook: it will become a valuable document.

Now each of these big organizations tend to 'carve up' Britain into their territories. Thus there is no point in writing to, say, Courage to ask about a pub in an area that is a Scottish & Newcastle stronghold. Obvious? Yes, but people do just that sort of thing – hardly a good way of impressing a future employer as to your knowledge of his trade. Of course, you do get overlaps among the big brewers – Bass, for instance, may have pubs cheek-by-jowl with Whitbread, but I have tried to stress that it is essential you find out all this information for yourself and not rely purely on letters fired off in the random hope that they find the right office eventually. Having once determined the major brewers in your chosen area you can easily find out their regional headquarters, simply by asking a tenant or manager of a pub or even looking it up in the local telephone directories.

Secondly, make a note of the smaller, independent breweries which own pubs. You may find three or four in any area. Some will be known to you, others total mysteries. Spend some time looking at those pubs. Are they well kept? Do they seem welcoming? Could you see yourself as a tenant in such a place? If you like the look of what you see, take yourself off to the brewery concerned and ask at reception if you could talk to their tied-house manager, or the equivalent, to find out what your chances might be if you were to apply. If they issue preliminary forms, take one and say you will send it on. Sometimes you will be treated in an off-hand, uninterested manner. Make up your own mind about this. But I know what my feelings would be: if I were poorly received I would reckon that that brewery was poorly managed and not worth pursuing. If their own front-of-house manner was off-hand then that attitude percolates down from the top, not up from the bottom, and will be reflected in all their dealings, especially with their tenants who, remember, are 'tied'.

During your chats with landlords you will also discover a great deal of local lore and rumour about other pubs and landlords, and other breweries. Keep an ear open for movements in the trade which may affect your future. I mentioned in a previous chapter that breweries are not run any longer by brewers, but by accountants, to whom tenant welfare or well-being is of no consideration at all. Thus a boardroom may well decree one day that some, if not all, of its most profitable houses will no longer be tied but managed, meaning even greater profits, they hope; whereas the less profitable will be sold off as free houses or, in a distressingly cynical attitude, left empty once the present tenant has received his marching orders via the non-renewal of his lease, and then be delicensed, to be sold 'with potential for improvement as a private dwelling'. This is by no means uncommon as it prevents any pub becoming a success under individual ownership and challenging others still in brewery hands. But sometimes even the biggest breweries make mistakes and instead of closing down pubs they have sold them off as working, if unprofitable, properties to individuals whose own hard work and flair have made them runaway successes in two or three years.

Finding an Opening with a Brewery
This business of looking around will be acutely depressing and many times you will feel like giving up, either because you cannot find a brewery with any vacancies for tenants or managers or because no free houses of any sort, let alone ones which might appeal to you, seem about to come on to the market. But do not despair. This is a very large step you are going to take with your future and caution has to be the watchword. In any event, do you really believe that just because you have made up your mind what to do then the right openings magically appear? Not at all. Not in any sphere of life. The point is: research is never wasted. For tied or managed houses get your name known to the breweries, get your serious intentions into the minds of the right department heads. Keep at it. I know there is an awfully long waiting-list for pubs in many areas and you are apparently right at the bottom of it. OK, but things change quickly and no brewery which sees an opportunity of making more profit through you, as opposed to someone else, is going to worry about whether you joined their waiting-list yesterday or two years ago. In fact it could be said that the chap who 'joined' two years ago has not actually made much of an impression. The business is highly competitive throughout and nowhere more so than in the hunt for a decent pub from a tenant's point of view or by the brewery for just the right person to fill a forthcoming vacancy.

As an example, long before I ever entered the licensed trade I remember being a guest speaker at some Friday

evening function and sitting throughout dinner next to
the tied-house director of a well-known brewery.
Although the function was in no way connected with the
trade I did have a few harsh things to say about pubs in
general, both in my speech and in normal conversation
with this man. Much to my surprise, at the end of the
evening, he gave me his card and wrote on it the name of a
somewhat down-at-heel pub which we had discussed
earlier.

'If you ring me by 5 o'clock on Monday that pub can be
yours,' he told me. 'I like your ideas and they would suit
that house.'

I told him I would think about it but on the Monday
rang him and declined his offer.

'You're a fool,' he said. 'We're going to spend a lot of
money on that place and you would have been the chap to
run it.'

We parted amicably enough, but some years later I
chanced by that particular pub and indeed it had been
transformed into very much the sort of pub I had
envisaged. It looked welcoming and very attractive with
nicely laid-out grounds. All the filthy tumble-down
outbuildings had been cleared away and careful restor-
ation of the ancient structure had been enhanced by good
lighting and good signs. It was obviously very busy and
successful, with good food and an up-market clientele, all
the things I had presumptuously told him could be done.
Although I did not regret my earlier decision the story
serves to illustrate the point about waiting-lists, applica-
tions and so on. The simple fact is that this chap thought I
was the right landlord for that particular pub at that time
because I had fired him with my ideas (which probably
coincided with his own anyway) and seemed capable of
carrying them out. Let it be a lesson to you. You may not
be lucky enough to sit next to the right chap at a dinner, as
I did, but once you get into his office you have just the
same chances as anyone else. It is up to you to give him
the impression that you are the only one worth listening
to.

If you are looking for a tied house or a managed one,
quarter the chosen area and apply to every brewery within

that area. But please do not just apply and leave it at that. You must have something to contribute too, not just in money by any means, but in ideas, drive, initiative. Do not worry about the opposition – make certain your application to a brewery is much better than anyone else's. After all, why should they take you in preference to some other applicant? Because you are going to be a better bet, that's why. And you are not going to be able to prove that without some very persistent and steady persuasion.

Now most of the big breweries are open and honest in their dealings with applicants and will frequently set an accurate and sensible figure, specifying exactly how the amount has been calculated. Purely as an example a brewery might say to a prospective tenant that the ingoing will be £24,000. This figure may be arrived at as follows:

Value of outgoing tenant's fixtures and fittings	£10,000
Value of stock at take-over	2,500
Sum set aside for repairs, decorations, dilapidations etc.	5,000
Quarterly rental to brewery	2,500
Brokers/Valuation fees	1,500
Security deposit to brewery	2,500
	£24,000

Now it should be borne in mind that if you are dealing with a reputable brewery there will be no 'hidden charges' in their ingoing estimates. The total will cover everything you need to set up in business and continue for the next three months, by which time, it is to be hoped, you will have made enough money to cover your liquor purchases and sufficient profit to cover your overheads and the rent when it next becomes due.

Ingoing costs depends entirely on the type of pub, its position, size and so on. Some properties are available for the sort of figure I mention above but it is unlikely that any newcomers to the trade, however, would be offered a tenancy valued at a £100,000 or more. At least not until inflation makes even £100,000 seem cheap.

The smaller breweries are often less choosy about their tenants, or less well able to choose as carefully or scientifically, since they do not have large departments staffed with experts in personnel selection. Nor will they be quite so accurate (or demanding) about their ingoing figures, so you must make quite sure about the type of brewery you are dealing with. Nothing can be more dangerous than not having enough capital, it is true, but it is even more depressing to discover all sorts of 'extras' which need more and more money. The big breweries guarantee that the figure they give you at the start will be the one to start you in business for real. And, another plus point, their local staff are trained in 'hand holding', which means that you can summon help whenever you run into a problem. For the most part brewers' reps are not only very pleasant, but also a fount of good advice, and if they cannot help, they will soon get someone from head office to come along to sort out anything that troubles you.

Free-House Hunting

Free houses are to a much greater extent an open money market where, for the most part, the chap with the biggest cheque gets the property. But not always. Some pubs belong to family estates, or perhaps a trust, and they may well be offered to people whose ideas and plans are sympathetic to those of the family or trustees, and would be highly acceptable to that area. In such cases the 'right' people are more important than the money they have in the bank.

Now it is true that such places are not all that common, but believe me they do exist and you find them just as you would find other free houses – through local newspaper property notices or in advertisements in specialist magazines like *Caterer & Hotelkeeper*. But as an introduction to the whole business you should also bear in mind the *Morning Advertiser*, which is the daily newspaper of the licensed trade and is owned by the National Association of Licensed Victuallers. Even if you bought or borrowed only one or two copies of this paper (it is not always easily obtainable in some parts of Britain) you would get an immediate 'feel' of the whole industry, from its major problems to its small, pettifogging news items. For sheer diversity, bearing in mind that the *Morning Advertiser* only carries news of interest to publicans and the drinks business, you will be amazed by what goes on. Its advertisement pages cover every aspect of the business, from jobs vacant and wanted to large licensed premises for sale. Whether you continue to take the paper is up to you but I do advise you to study what you can when you can.

In addition to the advertisements in local and national publications, there are a great number of brokers – that is, estate agents – who specialize in the buying and selling of public houses. Some of them even deal with brewery tenancies. But once again you will find out who they are through their advertisements in the trade press.

If you are after a free house then it is a good idea to register with one or more of these agents, just as you would with any estate agent if you wanted to buy a dwelling house. For the most part, these agents are efficient and honest and frequently have what is called a 'hot box', a list of prospective buyers well known to them, who are waiting for just the right sort of premises. This means that some suitable pubs never actually appear 'on the market' but are sold within days to clients registered with them. This of course facilitates the whole process and also leads to the seller being charged less than would otherwise be normal, as no advertising is required nor time wasted.

Of course, it is unlikely that you, as a first-time buyer, will be so specific as to your requirements that you can be 'matched' in such a way, but you really must try to be as accurate as possible in what you want, and how much you have to spend, to avoid wasting their time as well as yours. For the most part, brokers are very skilled at pricing licensed properties, probably far more accurate than normal estate agents, and they are well worth listening to as their advice is often sound and based on years of experience of pubs.

Assets and Liabilities
It must be obvious that to a certain extent the question of available money, your own realizable assets, in other words, will determine the sort of public house you are

likely to get. Thus your first task is to set out, on paper, the exact details of what you are worth in terms of assets and what your indebtedness is in terms of liabilities. It will look something like this:

Assets
Value of house
  contents
  personal possessions
Second car, caravan
Second home
Building society account
Investments, National
  Savings, stocks and
  shares etc.

Liabilities
Mortgage
Overdraft or bank loans
Hire purchase
Outstanding bills, debts etc.
Other commitments, school
  fees

You must be honest with yourself and include everything, even such things as perhaps some jewellery your wife might have been left in a will. Remember, it is what you are *worth* in financial terms that you must arrive at, whether you propose selling items or not. Having done that sum, keep it by you. You will probably be depressed at how little you are worth. But do not worry – there is still a place for you in the licensed trade, if you know where and how to look.

So I think it best to set out exactly the meanings of the terms which I have already used, like tied, free house, managed and to explain as simply as possible the system under which they operate. Remember: a thorough under-standing of what is available to you as a putative landlord will stand you in good stead and will also help you to decide which system is better for you, notwithstanding the question of money. You would be surprised at the number of people applying to breweries, or even contemplating buying a pub of their own, who are completely ignorant about the whole background to the trade.

Raising the Capital
Now what will it cost, this free house? Well, in any book

prices are invidious, for obvious reasons, but a rough guide of what you should expect to pay for a free house is its annual turnover plus a sum for the living accommodation, grounds, potential and so on. You must understand that pubs are not like 'lock-up' shops – you are buying both a business and living quarters, often quite extensive, and you cannot expect to pay less than the local going rate for the 'private' side of the building just because it is attached to a 'public' house. But do not be too dismayed by this. The value of living areas and so on may not be all that great, especially if you have to spend a lot of money on making the business viable, in the case of a run-down pub, or more profitable in the case of a pub which is not trading anywhere near its potential. However, remember that you are essentially buying a business and if it is within or near a popular catchment area and trading profitably the asking price will be in six figures, particularly if you have seen it advertised in a publication like the *Caterer & Hotelkeeper*. This is not always true of pubs offered in local papers and these are most often the more suitable for the first-time publican.

It also fair to say, despite my somewhat jaded remarks earlier in this chapter, that breweries from time to time wish to sell pubs, particularly if they are run-down, would cost too much to do up, or are simply 'surplus to requirements'. You must obviously be careful that you are not being conned, for breweries are efficient salesmen, but the same is true of most organizations as well as many private property owners, so providing you have done your research properly you may well find yourself with a bargain, especially in country areas. Once again, the pages of the *Morning Advertiser* or the local weekly paper will help to keep you informed.

But having found your free house, how do you raise the money?

Well let me say from the start that you are doomed to failure if you mortgage yourself up to the hilt and have no spare capital. Whereas the major breweries, as we saw in Chapter 3, take into account the 'working capital' they reckon you will need, private buyers are often very foolish and enter a property without a single penny piece to spare. So in your calculations you must make sure you have a reasonable sum left over from your estimated ingoings to keep you going for, let us say, a minimum of three months. Three months? Yes, at least. And preferably six months to a year. For there is a simple fallacy about most businesses, the licensed trade in particular, which is that if you buy, say, a barrel of beer and sell it for a profit you will have the cost price to buy you the next barrel and the profit you have made to help with other things. Absolutely watertight as an argument; absolutely wrong in practice. There will be so many demands for your money from so many sources that you will wonder where on earth the hoped-for profit has gone. It will quite possibly be a long time before you make a recognizable profit, assuming, that is, that you have bought a lowly pub with your money and not some vast going concern in which you either sit back and let it chunter on or seek ways of increasing the amount of money it will yield you. I can well remember, after two despairing years of trying to make a go of a certain pub, being told by our accountant that contrary to all advice and expectation we had made a profit of £2,000 and were well on the way to substantial success. It certainly did not appear that way to my wife and me, but it does demonstrate the importance of a good accountant who can stand back from a business and see which way it is going – often the wretched owners are run too ragged to distinguish the wood from the trees. We shall return to this subject later on.

But if you do not have sufficient money for your ideal pub, how do you set about raising the necessary? With great difficulty, is the smart answer. The licensed trade in Britain is not viewed with the greatest favour by lending institutions, especially if the licensee has no track record in the business. So your main aim is going to have to be one of convincing a prospective lender that his money is not only safe but guaranteed a return without problems.

Impressing the Money Men

To this end thorough preparation is essential as you will have to make a 'presentation' setting out your own financial situation (for example, how much money of your own you intend to invest in the new venture), as well as the amount of extra capital required and, of extreme importance, why and what it is for. Just as we saw in the section dealing with breweries how tenants have to set out their plans and forecasts for any pub offered to them, so you will have to do the same in the case of a free house but in a much more thorough manner. It may not be easy at this stage to do detailed cash-flow forecasts and so on, but because you must appear as *professional* as possible to anyone who might lend you money it is a task you have to undertake, however convinced you are that it is merely an exercise in crystal-ball gazing. How can anyone, I hear you ask, forecast such a thing as a flow of cash when no such commodity as yet exists?

I know it may seem somewhat puzzling but it is a thing understood by bankers and money-men and is not quite as daft as it sounds. In the first place you will almost certainly know, or be able to guess pretty accurately, some of the expenses you are going to have to meet in the pub you have set your heart on. Well, you already have some definite base. Many expenses, I admit, will be 'guesti-mates'. Do not worry, the money-men know all these things and understand them. So if you are realistic and above all, sensible, they will appreciate your efforts. If you are silly then they will see that too, and mark you down as unreliable. That would be fatal to your future chances.

To give you an idea of what a typical cash-flow forecast should look like I have set it out in the form of a table (1) and then filled in, albeit a little arbitrarily, some typical figures. By taking a little time to examine the figures I think you will see what I am driving at. For instance, in June I have inserted a sum of £5,000 as expenditure on equipment. Now this could be for new cellar stillages, storage racks, refrigeration or cooling shelves, perhaps a new cooker for the kitchen. It increases your overdraft demands dramatically and the bank manager may refuse such a hoist, or may caution against the total. But at the same time it has already performed a useful function, for the end-of-year figures may be better than you forecast, in which case he will be a lot more ready to help you.

I have also put in some other pointers. Receipts on food

Table 1

Cash-flow Forecast

Month	Jan	Feb	Mar	Apr	May	June	July	Aug	Sept	Oct	Nov	Dec
Bank Balance/OD	nil	6.95	4.6	3.25	1.90	.79	[5.36]	[5.66]	[5.01]	3.91	2.81	3.92
PAYMENTS												
Equipment	2.00	1.00	.40	nil	.10	5.00	nil	.25	nil	.10	nil	.05
Suppliers:												
Food	.50	1.00	.60	.80	1.01	1.10	1.20	1.00	1.00	.80	.60	1.15
Drink	1.00	.50	.50	.90	.85	1.50	.95	.80	.70	.60	.30	1.10
Wages	.75	.70	.60	.75	.75	1.00	1.00	1.00	1.00	.90	.75	1.00
Overheads	.50	.50	.50	.80	.50	.50	.60	.60	.60	.60	.60	.70
VAT										1.71		
Maximum borrowings (As required)	[4.75]	nil	nil	nil	[1.31]	[8.31]	[9.11]	[9.31]	[8.31]	[6.91]	[6.77]	[7.92]
RECEIPTS												
Own capital	10.00											
Sales:												
Food	.90	.65	.70	.85	1.15	1.60	1.90	2.10	2.30	2.10	1.55	2.85
Drink	.80	.50	.55	.90	.95	1.35	1.55	1.95	2.10	2.00	1.30	2.30
VAT				.15				.25				
Closing Balance:	6.95	4.60	3.25	1.90	.79	[5.36]	[5.66]	[5.01]	[3.91]	[2.81]	[3.92]	[2.77]

Note: Figures in £s 000. Square Brackets = Deficit

and drink show a marked decline in February and March, again in October and November. Those are the trade's traditional 'dead' or 'shoulder' months. In the summer, by contrast, the receipts show a healthy increase. But so do your expenses if you look under 'wages'. 'Balance' is a term frequently used in all accounting work; in the case of your cash flow, the word has a slightly different meaning: try to make your cash flow as 'balanced' month by month as possible. You may well be surprised just how accurate the forecasts turn out to be.

In Chapter 11 we shall take a look at most other aspects of money management and book-keeping but having considered a cash-flow forecast here it would make sense to draw up a profit and loss forecast at the same time. Once again it seems to be yet another exercise in pointless speculation – how can anyone forecast a profit or a loss before a single penny has been spent on anything? I quite understand, but just get on with it.

In Table 2 I have inserted, again arbitrarily, various figures to give you an idea of the layout. It is, bear in mind, an exercise designed to give you a better idea of what money your pub needs to earn in order to cover all your outgoings. In this profit and loss forecast, however, you will notice that VAT has not been included. To do so was necessary in the Cash Flow (it forms part of what the table purports to be, after all – money going in and out) but if VAT is included in your profit and loss the resulting figures will be misleading.

I have, however, tried to keep the two tables more or less in parallel by keeping to the same figures, but in reality you must reduce the amount of your sales receipts by 15% VAT in Table 2 to give your true financial position.

It does not take a financial wizard to see from this table that a better-than-break-even point occurs around August and continues, with only one slight 'hiccup' in November. In reality I think I am being over-optimistic on your behalf but if the forecasts are at all accurate (and, once again, they may well be surprisingly so), there is some very definite information upon which any lender can judge the

Table 2

Profit and Loss Forecast

Month	Jan	Feb	Mar	Apr	May	June	July	Aug	Sept	Oct	Nov	Dec
SALES	1.70	1.15	1.25	1.75	2.10	2.95	3.45	4.05	4.40	4.10	1.85	5.15
less COSTS												
Food	.50	.80	.60	.80	1.01	1.10	1.20	1.00	1.00	.80	.60	1.15
Drink	1.00	.50	.50	.90	.85	1.50	.95	.80	.70	.60	.30	1.10
Wages	.75	.70	.60	.75	.75	1.00	1.00	1.00	1.00	.90	.75	1.00
Gross profit/loss	[.55]	[.85]	[.45]	[.70]	[.51]	[.65]	.30	1.25	2.70	1.80	.20	1.90
Overheads	.50	.50	.50	.80	.50	.50	.60	.60	.60	.60	.60	.70
Net profit	[1.05]	[1.35]	[.95]	[1.50]	[1.01]	[1.15]	[.30]	.65	1.10	1.20	[.58]	1.20

Note: Figures in £s 000. Square Brackets = Deficit

position for himself.

A word of warning, however. Neither forecast takes any heed of your own living costs, nor does it deal with loan interest/repayments. You will have to make provision for such things from your own knowledge, and I also advise you to get a proper accountant to help you draw up such tables for your final presentation. The better it is the greater the chance of getting that pub you so dearly want.

Now in some instances the brokers selling the property may in fact have access to funds, and at a reasonable price, in other words – interest. You will see advertisements for such a service in magazines like the *Caterer & Hotelkeeper, Morning Advertiser* and so on. But do not expect the interest to be the same as you would pay to a building society which, is must be said, will under no circumstances lend money on public houses as such, although they may consider the living quarters to be sufficient security to allow them to advance money. Building societies exist solely to help people who require a residential roof over their heads; they are not in the business of helping businesses. And just bear in mind that for all business lending the going interest rate is at least one and probably more than two percentage points above normal mortgages. But failing 'in-house' finance deals, you have recourse only to the open market, and you may just as well start with the high-street banks.

Now as I said earlier financial institutions always get a little sniffy about lending money on premises connected with alcohol. I think it must be something to do with the general hypocrisy of the British towards anything pleasurable, but it is nonetheless important to visit the manager of a bank local to the pub you have your eye on. The manager will know all sorts of things about trading conditions on his own patch and may even know a considerable amount about that particular pub and why it is doing well or not. I remember when we were searching for a country pub years back we asked to see a manager of a bank in the local market town who, it rapidly became embarrassingly obvious, handled the account for the pub concerned. The manager was a model of tact, but we gained the strong impression that that particular pub in that particular location was doomed to failure from the start. So we finally asked him the one question that you should always ask any bank manager from whom you are trying to glean information.

'All things being equal, would you lend money on that business?'

If the manager says no then accept his word. It is highly unlikely any other lending institution will, or certainly not at a reasonable rate of interest.

Of course the whole question of borrowing money often revolves around how much. A high-street bank may well consider a few thousand is a reasonable investment if it is, say, for working capital and the bulk of the money is being put in by the borrower. But it is unlikely to be attracted if money is being raised from all over the shop, at varying rates of interest. So the important thing is to make sure your presentation deals with all these matters, however minor some of them may seem, so that a prospective lender can see exactly what the situation is and where he or she stands. 'Deals' of this nature can be arranged, but only in circumstances of patent honesty – in which case it is always worth while approaching one of the banks at the start.

It may also be worth while here to utter a word of warning about the increasingly popular 'low-start' schemes, by which banks and other lenders offer money at interest rates about two or three per cent below current market rates for, say, the first three years. Naturally the idea is attractive – who wouldn't prefer to pay a fixed, low rate of interest until they were on their feet with a successful business and a healthy cash flow behind them? The problem is that the difference between the low rate and the market rate has to be financed somehow, normally by what is called a 'roll-up' arrangement. In this system the unpaid interest is added on to the capital sum, which then attracts interest at the market rate. This can lead to nasty shocks all round, especially if the business is not able to absorb such a considerable hoist in repayments. So it is better to regard these schemes as helpful only if the business you are buying could realistically stand full mortgage interest repayments *from the outset*. If it could, then you can go for 'start-up' schemes with confidence, as it will give you much needed financial leeway and allow your 'surplus' money to be spent on improvements or ideas to increase your profitability, which in turn will allow you to face the realities of the eventual greatly increased interest/capital repayments with a certain amount of equanimity.

Whatever you do, however, you must try to deal with lenders who know about the licensed trade, who have an interest in it beyond the making of a swift buck and whom you can impress with your own innovative ideas and fresh approaches. You not only have to sell yourself but sell your knowledgeable enthusiasm. Lenders are not short of calls on their money. You just have to persuade them to let you have it rather than someone else.

Leaseholds
Finally, after brewery tenancies and free houses, we should take a look at leases, either from family or national trusts or estates which own licensed premises as part of large land holdings.

There are a lot more leasehold properties available than you might at first think, though as I suggested earlier in this chapter they can be difficult to find and even more difficult to secure. An obvious source is the National Trust itself, which within its land holdings own the freeholds of a number of pubs, inns, hotels and even restaurants. Some of these are managed, it is true, but from time to time leaseholds do come on the market although the terms may not suit every applicant, the National Trust, for many people, having a deeply unimaginative and bureaucratic reputation.

In fact, of course, it would be a very foolish person altogether who accepted any lease from any landlord without first getting the advice of a very smart lawyer, smarter than the legal experts who draw up leases. Remember, there is no such thing as a good landlord. Good tenants, yes, certainly. But good landlords, never. So you must make absolutely certain what the terms are before you sign anything and if you, or your lawyer, has the slightest doubt or query which is not satisfactorily answered then do not hesitate – pull out and let the place go to some other fool, however attractive it may seem at first sight.

As an example, some years ago we were offered the lease of a pub which seemed, to us, perfectly acceptable and in order, and although naturally enough we let our lawyer see it we regarded it as a mere formality. Thank goodness we did. For carefully hidden in the lease was the infamous clause which gave the landlords – in this case a publicly known and 'respected' Trust – the right to sell the property themselves should we ever wish to leave within the 35-year initial term, and without our getting a single penny. This clause (carefully couched in legal jargon not easily under-stood by the layman, as it is intended to be) is a common 'try on'. In effect, it allows an incoming licensee to work his fingers to the bone building a business up, apart from property improvements and so on, and then, instead of being able to sell it himself and reap the benefit of his work and expertise, the lessors can step in and pocket all the money – a system actually less morally defensible than any normal brewery tenancy agreement. I feel I should also mention that leaseholds are not viewed favourably by the high-street banks in terms of collateral security for loans and, indeed, in Scotland there is absolutely no chance of a bank lending money on any lease.

In the case of ordinary, honest leases deprived of the attentions of bright lawyers there should really be very few complications apart from the length of the lease, the period between rent reviews and the inevitably conten-tious question of 'repairs'. Let us deal with the last question at once.

Most leases are 'full repairing', which should mean that with the exception of the basic structure of the building all ordinary maintenance is the responsibility of the lessee. But what is 'ordinary maintenance'? In a great many cases an incoming tenant can take over an almost derelict building and find himself having to put the whole premises back into habitable order at his own expense. So just make sure – and get your lawyer to make sure – who pays for what. And do not accept word of mouth or promises, however genial the landlord or his agent may seem. No landlord is interested in anything other than the rent and will do as little as possible to deserve it. It is a matter for the legal eagles, not for you, to argue. With everything in black and white there can be no mistaken impressions, burned fingers and out-of-joint noses, and as a result both parties should end up, if not happy, at least in a state of an amicable armed truce.

Most decent leases are for a period of up to thirty-five years, especially in the case of older and perhaps run down properties and businesses. This gives the lease-holder a chance to build up the business, improve the property within his own obligations or requirements and then have something of value to sell on, without let or hindrance, to another tenant, who should still find it worth while paying quite a considerable sum for the whole project. This does not mean, of course, that you will be expected to sell, or even perhaps want to. And you may wish to renew the lease at the end of the initial term. If you have been a good tenant most landlords will be only too happy to renew the lease, but you could be unlucky and, during the last five years of your lease, face the prospect of losing your home and business without a penny to show for all the work. That is why most lessees are cautious and look around for a buyer while their lease is still worth something. Either that, or get a firm agreement that renewal is a mere formality.

It is usual for a rent review to be every five years, though with some leases it may be three. This increase (for such it will inevitably be) should be in line with the cost-of-living index, and if no agreement can be reached between landlord and tenant it is normal for an independent assessor to arbitrate, his financial estimate being binding on both parties. This provision is included in all proper lease agreements. The main problem arises in those cases where you, the tenant, have spent considerable sums upgrading the property, obviously with the enthusiastic consent, if not financial assistance, of the landlord. I was once told by a very senior surveyor who had spent much of his life dealing with leasehold public houses that it is virtually impossible separately to assess improvements made to any property by the leaseholder, because of the 'knock on' effect to the property generally. Thus you may have spent a lot of money in improvements only to have them assessed as being of considerable value to the landlord in terms of increased rent. And that is the rent you will have to pay. Thus even more care is needed with the details of the lease before you sign it. In an ideal world, all structural alterations and improvements should be undertaken by the landlord, who can then claim a fair rent return, after having carried them out at the tenant's request or in accordance with his agreement. This is not always possible (such landlords are few and far between) so you will almost certainly be faced with a less-than-ideal compromise, like most other tenants of leasehold property. If it is any comfort the problems you have as a leaseholder will be common to a great many others, and I do feel I should point out that in practice the picture is not quite as black as I have appeared to paint it. But just be certain *before* you sign anything, that's all. Afterwards is too late for complaints.

5 *Ground Rules*

So much for the problems of finding a pub and raising the money. You will already have learned something of the complexities, but now let us get through the doors and see what happens. But once again – is it your pub, that is, a free house, or does it belong to a brewery? It can make a big difference.

Moving In – Free Houses
Let's first suppose you have a free house. Straight off, this means you have a free hand about whether you stay open or close for a day or two while the change-over takes place. My advice to you is simple: close. Life will be hellish if you do not.

Now, of course, if you do close you have made sure your predecessor will have announced the fact beforehand, in plenty of time. And you will also have made sure that the actual moving-out/moving-in arrangements have been discussed, planned and agreed in the minutest detail between both of you, removal firms, drinks suppliers and so on. You have also made sure your banking needs and system have been set up, along with notification to the Customs and Excise (for VAT registration); that you have set in train compliance with the Business Names Act; and, perhaps most important that you have what is called a Protection Order from the local magistrates which will allow you to sell alcohol when you do open. Now we shall look at all these complexities later, but I just wanted to stress that taking over a pub is not as easy as all that and that your problems are only just beginning. (You might have been forgiven for thinking most of them had been solved by getting the place in the first instance!)

But even if you shut to ensure all these myriad details are properly handled you will still get people who will wander in from the street, either genuinely ignorant of the change-over, or just trying it on. Now here is the second bit of advice: begin as you mean to go on. You may be running a public house, but it is also a private one too. Make no exceptions, whoever may be calling. You are shut until tomorrow, or the next day or whenever and there is a notice on the front door to that effect. Be absolutely firm, though polite and apologetic. The first sight of you, the new landlord, must give every customer an exact idea of how you are going to run the place. If necessary, keep the doors locked unless furniture is being moved in or out. The only exceptions to this entry bar might be the brewery or drink reps, who often call to collect cheques in settlement of their accounts on that last day and will try to 'sign you up' to ensure that you, the new landlord, continue to buy his firm's products. Do not, however, be rushed into anything. Ask them to call back in a day or so, when *you* are ready to see them. They will, without fail. A free house is a prized customer to any brewer or drinks supplier, so just be careful how you dispense your favours until you have had time to think about it and, above all, heard what the reps have to say in peace and quiet.

The advantages of closing for at least two days are fairly obvious. Day one will be the day your predecessor moves out. It will also be the day the trade valuer does his stock-take and assesses how much you owe the previous landlord for his wet stock, glassware, cleaning materials, furniture, fittings and so on. Once this sum is agreed it *must* be paid at once, without quibble. This transaction is quite separate to the settlement payable on the property itself, which is a matter arranged between the respective solicitors, as in all property deals. The valuer will also apportion his own charges, which must be paid there and then.

Now you will sometimes be advised to have your own valuer in attendance, going round in tandem with your predecessor's valuer. In certain cases, perhaps, such a procedure may be desirable, though I cannot think where or when unless the outgoing landlord is a crook and prone to employing crooks. By far the better course is to agree to employ the same valuer, and to abide by his valuation. These men are for the most part understanding and honourable. They tend to be quick, efficient and skilled and their charges are laid down in advance. It is customary for you and the outgoing landlord to hand him your own cheques, divided equally in settlement of his account, and for you to hand a further cheque to your opposite number in settlement for the stock and so on. Providing the solicitors have also done their work, the pub is now yours, irrevocably, and as a gesture you are now entitled to move behind the bar (your own bar, remember!) and offer both of them a drink 'on the house', along with their families.

But one word of warning: make it clear to the valuer in advance that when it comes to what is called 'wet stock' you are only prepared to pay for stuff which is actually drinkable. If in doubt about the sort of landlord you are buying from, perhaps because his business is running down or he has lost interest in it you may be paying for some pretty worthless goods – as I did once, discovering to my dismay that more than £400-worth had to be tipped down the drain the moment my predecessor departed. Not a good way to start out on any new venture and a painful example of that motto you must regard as absolutely essential in all matters regarding drink and food: 'If in doubt, chuck it out.'

Now the day of actual settlement is a matter for agreement between the two parties. It is probably best if the valuer does his rounds after your opposite number has actually moved out of the premises, and before you have moved anything of yours in. This avoids any misunderstandings over the inventory, or doubts and possible arguments about who owns what. Such an agreement makes it easier all round, quite apart from avoiding the appalling consequences of having one set of furniture-removers coming downstairs with the marriage bed while another set are on their way up.

In any event, the whole process is one of abject misery, far worse than any ordinary household move you have ever suffered. The pub you have set your heart on will suddenly look tatty, wrecked and forlorn. Even if the outgoing landlord has really gone to town with the dustpan and brush (few do, alas) there will still be mountains of rubbish stacked outside and so much work, not only in the bars and stock areas themselves but in your own living quarters, that even the stoutest resolve will weaken. If you have a family to help, or some good, capable friends, the task will be that much lightened and, afterwards, you may even be able to do as we have always done – have a drink and then sit down to a damn good evening meal. Whatever the tasks ahead, whatever the surroundings, it is the best tonic in the world.

You will have understood why I advise at least a two day closure: one for the other chap to move out and get all the valuations done, the next day for you to move in, or finish moving in, and prepare yourself for the shock of opening your own doors for the first time.

Moving In – Tied Houses

Let us now take a look at the change-over if it is a tied house. In this case the problems and miseries are compounded because breweries, who always want their pound of commercial flesh, actually dictate your exact opening and closing hours and even whether you can shut on, say, Christmas evening. The most latitude they will allow you is to close at lunchtime on change-over day, though even this is forbidden by some breweries.

The process of valuation will progress as usual, as will moving out and moving in. It is as well to bear another point in mind, when you go into a pub you will be obliged to buy everything the outgoing tenant includes in the inventory, albeit at a price agreed between your valuer and his. There will be no saying 'I don't want that', or 'that bit of brass is awful', you will have to buy it whether it is junk (in your opinion) or not.

One of the most frustrating things about being a tenant is the fact that when it is your turn to move on, even to retire, you will have personally very little to 'sell on'. In other words, you will have only your furniture and other bits and pieces, most of which you possibly bought from the previous tenant, plus the stock at valuation. You own nothing else. You do not even have 'goodwill' to sell as that is considered to belong to the brewery, however hard you have worked or for however long. In fact the money you are likely to receive has merely kept pace with inflation. It can be very disappointing. And nowadays, because of the new tenancy agreements I mentioned earlier, you could spend only a year or two in a pub, have to leave because the brewery thinks it has found a better tenant, and get back very little more than the original sum you put in. It may be sound business for the breweries but it is not very satisfactory for the tenant.

Opening Time
Well, having got straight, or as straight as you possibly can, time to open up. But what time? The whole of the 'permitted hours' – that is, 11 a.m. to 11 p.m. on weekdays – or just some of them? If you are the tenant of a tied house, the agreement will dictate such matters, but if the proud owner of a free house, what then? So here comes the third piece of advice. You should have decided this question long before you bought the place. And not only decided it, but promised yourself to stick to it. Never chop and change your times, other than extending them for certain permissible festivals. If you are in a very busy area like a town centre then you may decide to open all the time or, say, 11.30 a.m. to 3 p.m. and 5 p.m. to 11 p.m. If in the country, midday may be reasonable, and in the evening an opening hour of 7 p.m. may not come amiss. Your local researches will tell you what others do and whether some of the free houses are closed for a whole day, often a Monday, as many of them do in rural areas. Fix your times and stick to them. And if you are going to sell food, as we shall see in a later chapter, stick to those times too. Remember, local conditions will dictate your busiest times. Study those conditions and you will not go far wrong. You are in a 'service' industry. Try to serve the customers when they wish it not just when you do.

So, your doors are open. You will certainly be amazed by one factor. How busy you are. Yes, often packed out, especially if you have taken over a proper 'local' (town or country). All the old customers will be along to have a look at 'their' new landlord. By far the greater majority will not like what they see and compare you unfavourably, often to your face and certainly behind your back, to your predecessor. No matter that he watered the beer, had a foul tongue, was never known to say a kind word to anybody, served short measures and gave shorter change. All those attributes will suddenly be seen as virtues of a saint. 'Old so-and-so,' they will tell you with a chuckle, 'he was a proper card, he was. Mind you, you had to do as you were told. Ran a tight ship, did old so-and-so ...' and more along the same lines. Take no notice. Politely imply or, if necessary tell them, that this is no longer old so-and-so's pub but yours. You can add that he may be a hard or impossible act to follow, in which case you would not presume to emulate him, but that you propose serving your customers to the best of your ability and not someone else's. If you set off like that they may grumble initially, but you'll soon have them on your side.

And one other point. A great number of your customers will claim not only an intimate acquaintanceship with your predecessor but a deep and lasting friendship based on a regularity of custom so devoted that you are surprised the chap did not get valued among the fixtures and fittings. Beware. I bet the previous landlord never knew his name or would recognize him as having been there before, even if he did walk into the pub. Do not ask me why people claim this sort of thing but they do. I can remember believing a couple who went on at me like that soon after taking over a pub. They assured me that not only were they great friends with the former landlord, but that he had always made sure he had a stock of special canned beer for them, 'which is the only thing we drink'. So I too bought a case of their particular brew, not wishing to lose their custom. The cans from that case sat on a shelf for nearly three years, untouched. I gave them away to the local village fête eventually.

The fourth bit of advice? Listen to what people say. Do not give your own opinion about anything, do not encourage politics, religion or the death penalty as suitable subjects for discussion in your bar. Especially when you are new. Customers do not come to your bar to hear your thoughts or to ask your advice. They come to hear you agreeing with what they say. If you do that (if you have the eternal, sanctified patience to do that) and do it with a smile then you will be deemed to be both a paragon of virtue and a wise and brilliant conversationalist. Your fame will spread far and wide just by virtue of a pleasant greeting, a wise yet benign smile and a tongue rolled up tight, albeit far into your cheek. The chances of your actually achieving anything like what I say are remote. As a landlord you will quickly come to realize that you are to be the proud recipient of some of the most stupid, conceited, bigoted, crass, wrong, boring thoughts and opinions it has ever been any man's lot to hear. But do *not* do as I often did, and tell them so. It is a very quick way to lose a lot of trade. Almost as quick as that other cardinal sin, confiding to one customer your personal thoughts about another one. Keep those sort of opinions strictly within the family.

This spate of customers will only last for a day or two. After that you will start to wonder why you ever got into the business, for trade will dwindle, many of your regulars needing time to 'digest' their new landlord and in so doing may well do it in another pub. But take heart. For the most part they will return. You are beginning to see the Great British Public in a new light. But what may have seemed mutual hostility can easily turn into mutual respect and friendship and it is this factor which in time makes innkeeping such a worth while and enjoyable trade.

The fifth piece of advice is that, right from the start, you should resolve not to mention anything about alterations, improvements and redecorations. This makes customers feel uncomfortable. You will certainly be asked what you intend to do 'with the old place', even if you are a brewery tenant. I suggest you tread very warily and be non-committal, saying you need time to think if anything needs doing. As a word of warning, I was once asked even before taking an old and run-down country pub what I intended to do with it; to which I replied that I proposed knocking most of it down and building a twelve-storey hotel in its place. I thought it was funny, especially as the building was largely sixteenth century, as well as listed

and in a conservation village. But the joke was soured by
the inevitable rumour, which not only reached the rest of
the (horrified) village but even the planning authorities,
who curtly told me no such permission would ever be
granted. I replied that anybody who believed the tale I had
told them was a fool, but it nevertheless taught me a
lesson. There is no sense of humour in the British
countryside where 'their' pub is involved, even if a lot of
them never even enter the place.

Assistance from the Trade
I firmly believe that in no other trade or way of life is so
much genuine help and assistance there simply for the
asking.

It may seem strange but the licensed trade is quite
different to the catering trade. It is much jollier – I suppose
because it is so much more exposed to human fallibility. If,
say, you set about opening a restaurant no 'competitor'
would call round to offer help or advice. No traveller or
drinks supplier would say, 'Look, I'll give you a tip about
this ... or that'. And if such a person did offer advice on
how you should run your own restaurant you would
probably resent it and say 'What's it got to do with him?'
And can you imagine the chef of some superior hotel
running out of butter and just popping across the road to a
humble caff to borrow some? Or even less likely, the
owner of a humble caff popping into a smart restaurant
along the street to ask if he could borrow a dozen eggs? If
not unthinkable such 'sharing' is rare, to say the least. Yet
the pub trade is not like that at all. I can remember more
than once coming near to running out of certain mixers or
even spirits at holiday times when I had not bargained for
such a rush, ringing one or two local pubs to see if they
could help out and being told to collect what I wanted, or,
if I was busy, they would pop it round. When that does
happen, it is customary, as a matter of protocol, to replace
later what you have borrowed, and not pay for it, but you
must replace like with like, especially in the case of tied
houses.

You will have other landlords offering hints and tips
about awkward customers, local magistrates, police; about

where to get a better deal and from what wholesaler or retailer. They will warn of drink suppliers whose products are not competitive or not up to standard, and above all they will gossip (not necessarily maliciously) about others in the trade and their own problems. For the most part licensees are a pretty *sharing* lot and they will appreciate your problems and worries because they are, or were once, their own.

However, even though people are helpful, do try to be tactful. There is no harm at all in telling a landlord you are interested in having a pub in that part of the world and are honestly trying to 'pick his brains'. That is flattering and if he has time he will help you all he can, but make quite sure he is a reasonable chap first and then make sure he is not going mad trying to serve a full bar. As a landlord I got infuriated with people who tried to monopolize a conversation, or ask a string of questions when I was pulling pints, taking food orders and trying to add up complex rounds while still remembering to say good-morning or goodbye-and-thank-you to customers arriving or leaving.

Everyone else in the trade knows how awful it is to be open, fully lighted, warm, cosy, comfortable ... but without a single soul in the bar because it is snowing outside. They also know that the moment you give it up, turn out the lights, slam and bolt the front door, someone will hammer on it demanding a drink – someone, moreover, who will buy half a pint of the cheapest beer and sit over it until closing time without saying a word.

They will also know how such occasions can be swamped by the number of times the bar is packed with happy, chatting groups – groups who are tacitly telling you that they are having a good time and like being in your particular pub. Laughter and delight are then the order of the day and you realize that you are actually thoroughly enjoying yourself and would not change places with anyone in the world.

I can remember the first time we took a hundred pounds in one evening, the first time we took a thousand pounds in a week. I know that it was not a regular event every evening, or every week, but it was one mighty step in the right direction along what had been a rocky road.

Given a bit of luck, a load of good health and the hide, stubborn determination and unstoppable ambition of a rhinoceros out to catch a game warden, there is no reason why you should not succeed, and enjoy yourself in the process.

Apart from the customers coming in for a 'look-see' you will be inundated with brewery and drink reps or travellers selling everything and anything you can imagine. News of a change of licensee travels fast, as companies scan local papers to see who has been granted licensing protection orders by the magistrates. By far the greater number of reps are towers of strength, for you must recognize that they probably know far more about running a pub than you do yourself, course or no course. If in doubt about anything to do with the pub you eventually get, never hesitate to seek the advice of the reps.

They are, however, there to sell their company's products. They will not only be seeking to ensure their products are sold by you, but may also offer all sorts of blandishments in the way of loans for improvements and so on, knowing that any free-house owner is bound to be a bit strapped for cash. By all means consider what they tell you but just bear in mind that you have set off on too long and hard a road just getting a free house without chucking it away right at the start for what is, in effect, a brewery tie. Breweries do not offer money just because they are decent chaps. No, they want a return for it – such as a contract to take only their beer or a minimum quantity thereof, as well as other products. The term used, if you remember, is 'barrelage'.

And while we are talking about brewery reps, it is their (by no means unpleasant) custom to offer the landlord a drink whenever they call to see him. But so will a lot of other people, especially on day one. So be a bit careful. You will need a drink, believe me, but you will also need a clear head to last until at least 11 p.m. that night.

Accepting Drinks from Customers

Now my advice about accepting drinks from others is to set a monetary limit which is not too low to be offensive, but not too high to price out the humble customer who might one day suggest you 'have one on me'. I learned this trick a great many years ago when I used to help out the very popular landlord of a lovely Devonshire pub in the village where I then lived. In those days it was 'sixpennorth' or a 'tanner' (the old 6d). When my wife and I took a pub, we set it at 10p but customers complained, so we upped the ante to 20p. By the time you get your own pub it may well be, say, 50p.

The advantage of this system is that it is both fair and unlikely to upset anyone. Customers are very touchy about this issue and I am afraid the worst thing you can do is to say 'no', which is tantamount to a rude refusal to recognize the buyer as a friend. All you have to do, if you have a drink already – or you may have a rule that you never drink until a certain hour of morning or evening – is to take his money and put it in a container (we used an old glass) on a shelf where he can see it. I know that sounds silly. If you are to keep a pub, let me assure you it is not. The customer who offers you a drink, or the money for one, actually wants to see you either pour the drink or put the money in a special place from which it can be paid into the till when the times comes.

On the House?
And finally on this topic it is common practice (but by no means widespread) in some pubs for the incoming landlord to buy all his customers a drink the first morning or evening. Ask the previous landlord what you should do. In any event, it will do no harm as it is very cheap public relations. It should also be a rare occasion. It is not a good idea for landlords to buy customers drinks, and never 'in public', so to speak. There will be times, of course, when you will want to do just that, perhaps for some small favour or service a customer has rendered, but please make it discreet and never be tempted into too much generosity. I know that sounds mean but it is your living, remember, so never make a habit of buying even close friends a drink. If you worry about such a thing, look at this way: suppose you had a friend who was a bank manager, or perhaps a greengrocer. Would it ever occur to

you to go into the bank and expect him to say 'have a fiver on me'? Or into the chap's shop to hear him say 'have a sack of spuds on me'? Yet that is what you will be doing, by giving any Tom, Dick and Harry a drink. There will be times when it will be difficult, and obviously you must use your head, but friends who batten onto you are friends you are going to have to do without. You are in business to make money out of other people's conviviality, not yours. The true test of friendship (and you will discover, in your early days as an innkeeper, that you had far more 'friends' than you had ever believed possible) is a tacit understanding of your position and the business you are in.

Cashing Cheques and Credit
Earlier on I mentioned those customers who will claim faithful past attendance at your pub, as well as friendship with the previous landlord. Now by no means all of these are 'trying it on', but remember my oft-repeated adage 'start as you mean to go on', so be doubly careful when anyone asks for (or assumes you will give) credit or expects you to cash a cheque.

Actually the law does not allow credit to be given in pubs – an old attempt to stop the demon drink adding to the debt burden of working men or wastrels. This does not, however, apply to food, only alcohol. But the dividing line is a difficult one to tread – as is all licensing law – so until you are well established, perhaps with a thriving dining room and reliable local and business clientele, do not even consider any form of credit.

As regards cashing cheques, remember your bank will probably charge you at least 50p for every cheque paid in, so that if you cash a cheque for, say, a mere £5 you are losing ten per cent – an awful lot of money on the deal. Make it a firm rule not to cash personal cheques, at least at the start of your innkeeping life. You can do this quite pleasantly by pointing out to whoever asks that it will cost you 50p and suggesting that if they are really short they may care to make their cheque out for £5.50. You will discover that this immediately deters even the most determined, and providing you make the suggestion with a laugh then no harm will come by it. Alternatively, if you are going to be one of those wretched landlords who litter the place with those awful notices saying we don't do this or you mustn't do that then by all means get a cheap 'We don't cash cheques' from your local pub supplier. Such notices, to my mind, are a confession of incompetence on the part of any landlord, that or a disregard for the principles of handling the public, which is a crucial part of your job. Also bear in mind that those asking you to cash a cheque are very often among the better off in your local community, not 'dodgy' characters at all. On a personal note I can remember a very wealthy local man, retired but with a reputation for, shall we say, fiscal care, who asked me if to save him going to the bank I would cash him a cheque for £50 every Tuesday. My own bank manager fell about with laughter when I told him. 'Yes, go ahead,' he said. 'But charge him at least the 50p I shall charge you for handling the cheque, plus something for the trouble to you and convenience to him, plus a percentage of the money for petrol, parking, depreciation of his car and so on and see what he says. Otherwise tell him I'll sell him money, you stick to selling him beer.' I did indeed suggest, politely and cheerfully, to this customer that I could only do it on the terms my bank manager had suggested and after a bit of huffing and puffing all was forgotten and he remained a regular customer.

Finally, while still on the subject of cheques, always insist on writing your customer's cheque guarantee card number on the back of any cheque if that customer is settling a bill for, say, lunch and NEVER cash any cheque made out to someone else, even though the cheque is open and encashable. Landlords without number have been involved in police enquiries after cashing such cheques, so once again, make it a rule. Just to make things clear, however, I am not suggesting that you insist on seeing the cheque cards of known and reliable regular customers. Such would be a discourtesy, as it would be if such a person asked you to cash a cheque in an emergency. Just be careful and use your brains.

Friends and Undesirables
Now there is no question that your first days as a new
landlord may attract many of the sort of people you will
come to regard as friends. But remember – be careful of
'friends' in the bar. Do not ever be tempted to leave your
side of the bar to join people on the other side. The sight of
a landlord leaning against his own bar talking and
laughing exclusively with some of his personal mates has
lost more customers than he will ever realize. Of course
you can have friends, but your job is *behind your own bar*,
not in front of it, making *everyone* appear to be welcome
and treating all people in the same, friendly, genial
manner.

Ah, but I hear you murmur, how about the
undesirables? Yes, you will get some but once again, you
lay down the rules. You have a right to serve or not to
serve people, as you wish. There must rules of the house
(but not, please, a notice). You decide what rules suit you
and the type of pub you are running. The British, for
instance, are a sloppy, untidy race. Because of long years
and experience abroad, where neatness allows a man to
tread anywhere, we decreed that no one would be allowed
in our bar without a shirt, however hot the summer sun.
Only once did I ever have to ask anyone to put one on,
and when I did so I got an apology not only from the
young man himself but from his two mates who had been
repairing the road round the corner. They not only sent
him off to get his shirt, but they then all went to the gents'
to clean themselves up. You may think my attitude was
superior. You are wrong. The men came in every day for a
pint that week and we enjoyed serving them, and we also
subsequently saw two of them regularly in the evening or
at the weekend. But mind you, in our place they did have
somewhere decent to wash and brush up. That is not true
of a lot of pubs, so what can the publican expect? I firmly
believe that if you provide decent facilities in decent
surroundings you attract decent customers. Which leads
into another point.

I said the British are untidy. Actually, that word is too
mild. But what can you expect if outside most pubs
barrels, crates of empties, old rubbish bins, crushed

cardboard boxes and sacks of paper are piled high? Often by the front door. It is not just the British public which is mucky, the landlords are too. So what sort of greeting is that, to any pub? And what sort of customer can you expect to get? I will tell you: the one you deserve. If your pub proclaims to everyone by its outside appearance that you tolerate, nay, create a rubbish tip of your own by not stacking the detritus of your trade neatly and inconspicuously out of sight, then you are going to get the scruffy customers you deserve. You may say the British public do not notice such things. Well, they don't if they are that sort of person. But I can show you a dozen pubs in my part of the world that a great many customers never visit simply because the landlords do not care about their rubbish, anymore than they care about the smell of chips or stale beer, the lack of polish and cleanliness, and above all the lack of a welcoming smile and a pleasant 'good-morning'.

A Visit from the LVA

Very early on, perhaps your first day, you will probably get a visit from the secretary of the local branch of the Licensed Victuallers Association. He will almost certainly suggest you join and point out the many advantages of membership. Again, treat him as politely as you would an ordinary customer, but with the same reserve as you would any other chap trying to sell you something.

It would be wrong of me to try to persuade you one way or the other; whether you join or not is up to you, but remember the LVA is basically a protectionist organization which many people think has been somewhat tarnished by its attempt to ensure that only publicans should be entitled to sell alcohol – a battle long ago fought and lost, as evidenced by the high-street supermarkets and their liquor turnover. There are, in my opinion, precious few good reasons to be a member of the LVA (although they do run good retirement homes, I understand) but if you are in a tied house your brewery may expect it of you. Few free-house landlords are members, so far as my experience shows.

You will also receive visits from other landlords. Most of them you could do without, as they are there just to be nosey, to compare you well or ill with their own establishment and to heap often erroneous advice on to you. Most of them will be brash and insist on introducing themselves as though they were a circus act touting for business. You may like it. You may well be flattered. Your reaction is up to you and depends on your personality. Now and again you will come across rather quieter people, whom you will discover quite by accident are in the same trade. These were the people we liked having in our bar, and with many of them we have remained firm friends to this day. I say these things not because I want you to run your pub like I did mine, but to give you an idea of what to expect on your first day, or very soon afterwards anyway.

I have dwelt on the sort of people you can expect for a very definite reason. They are your bread and butter. We shall deal with the nitty-gritty in a later chapter, all the hard work which makes for the seven-eighths of running a pub which the public never see (and which, incidentally, they must never see, as it is not their concern).

6 Drink: the Dos and Don'ts

You may remember that in an earlier Chapter 1 said that people still go to pubs for beer. On the whole, that is the reason you are in this business and it is absolutely essential that the beer you keep and sell is always in the very best condition. So this chapter is about drink generally, yes, but first and foremost it is about beer. Your success or failure may well depend on it.

Now it has to be said that so far in this book I have not been particularly complimentary about breweries because they are now run largely by grey men called accountants whose knowledge of and interest in beer is at best limited and at worst minuscule. At one time, however, this was not so. Breweries were run by brewers and the head brewer was a man of august bearing and redoubtable knowledge. It is not so far from the truth today for, in every brewery, there is still a head brewer who is totally and solely devoted to the brewing of good ales. As a result (and because even accountants realize that beer is what keeps the company ticking over) the people who make the beer are as interested as the landlord of any pub to ensure that their product is sold only in first-class condition. To this end the breweries, their technical staff and their reps are 'on call' at all hours of the day to ensure that you are not only supplied with their product in first class condition but will get whatever help you need in looking after it and selling it.

This book is not the place for a treatise on brewing. However, assuming you are going to run a decent, ordinary pub in either town or country, and not some vast, amorphous road-house where neither licensee nor customer really cares about what he or she drinks, it is necessary to have some basic knowledge.

Real Ale and Keg Beer
What is rather pompously called 'real beer' or 'real ale' by pressure groups such as the Campaign for Real Ale (CAMRA), is in fact properly known as 'cask-conditioned'; that is, not pasteurized by heat treatment but racked off after a first fermentation to continue its second fermentation in barrels or casks in your cellar, until it is ready to be 'spiled and tapped' and drunk by (you hope) a grateful and often very appreciative public. No pressure is artificially incorporated and when served it should be 'a well-polished ale', as one of my customers used to call it – bright, clear and fragrant. It is, in reality, a living thing and because of that it needs careful storing and serving within a comparatively short time. There is no great 'trick' in serving it in perfect condition, whatever some publicans may say, but it does need proper and careful attention, and in this the brewery staff are expert and will do all they can to help and advise you.

This was not always so. A great many years ago, and because decent beer had become but a folk memory, owing to wartime restrictions and post war depression, the bigger breweries decided to phase out proper beer and introduce their newly discovered toy – keg beer. A beer which was gassy, pasteurized by the brewery and ready to serve the moment it reached any pub. Because it is essentially a 'dead' product its shelf life is very long. It does not have to be rolled onto stillages and left to settle, sometimes for two or three days, and within reason can be moved around even when it has been broached – something which would completely ruin a proper cask-conditioned beer. In addition, kegs take up less room in your cellar, standing upright rather than on their sides, and when needed you merely 'plug in' a special valve which incorporates the beer pipe to the bar and the pressure pipe from the CO_2 cylinder. The beer is ready to drink at once. The advantages were enormous, both to brewery and publican, largely because neither needed any longer to 'look after' their product to ensure its good condition. And when small, shelf-sized 'straight-through' refrigeration units came onto the market, thus ensuring that the pasteurized beer was served at the correct temperature demanded by the brewer, a whole vista of vast trouble-free profit opened up for the big breweries. There followed a clever manipulatory campaign by which the public at large were persuaded that they did not like the old type of beer (which had largely become undrinkable anyway) and that this new, keg beer had been provided specially for them. Within very few years, apart from some old-fashioned and very small, individual breweries, 'proper' beer had all but disappeared. The hiatus lasted for something like twenty years, or until an increasingly choosy public, with the money to indulge their wishes and the widespread ability to travel, began to question why the bigger breweries, already forming into vast conglomerates and controlling hundreds of pubs, failed to come up with as good a product as could be found in those establishments not part of any chain. To stay ahead of the game, or even in it, all breweries gave way and started once more to produce a decent, unpasteurized beer. Apart from Scotland, alas, where the gassy keg stills holds sway and a glass of decent ale is rarely obtainable.

With the rising popularity of cask-conditioned beers came the lager boom, largely among the young who found the traditional 'bitterness' of both cask and keg beers not completely to their liking. Lager is a pasteurized beer, yes, but it is fermented at a much lower temperature (and therefore more slowly) than traditional beers and English hops are not for the most part thought suitable. It is therefore a little more expensive, though just how much is an arguable point and some breweries would appear to be charging unreasonably for the product. As a landlord I was always surprised at the popularity of lager, both keg and canned. To me it never seems to taste remotely similar to the lager one drinks in Holland, Germany or Austria.

As I said, keg beer (and lager) needs little expertise and the cooler through which it is now passed is normally supplied, free of charge, by the brewery, although you will have to buy, perhaps at a specially reduced rate, or lease at a reasonable cost, a chilled display shelf upon which you can stack bottled beers and others drinks. The appearance and layout of those shelves are very much part of your marketing policy; customers like to see their favourite bottled drinks kept at a proper temperature and easily available.

In all matters to do with beers, however, cleanliness is absolutely essential. The cellar (or it may be just a coolish store-room, as in many pubs) must be kept spotless and washed out at least twice a week with a mild disinfectant – strong odours can taint beer, so be careful which brand you use. But as in all things to do with beer, your brewery reps will help and advise. Each brewery also recommends its own brand of cleaning agent for the beer pipes between cellar and bar. Cleaning these pipes, which attract deposits of yeast that cause further fermentation of beer, leading to cloudiness or 'fobbing' (excess foam), as well as an 'off' taste, must be done at least once a week and, if you are very busy or the weather hot, twice. It can be a tiresome task, which involves carefully mixing what is a very caustic solution, pumping or drawing it through the pipes after disconnecting them from the kegs or casks, letting the fluid 'stand' and then thoroughly flushing through with clean water. There is a saying that there is no such thing as bad beer, only bad publicans, and it is certainly true that by far the greatest number of complaints about beer are directly related to failure to clean the pipes regularly.

Nowadays, with modern attachments and gadgets, the business of cleaning pipes has become less of a chore, with multi-headed automatic systems to help with the cleaning, and even very gentle 'top pressure' gas pipes are now fitted to casks. These prevent air entering the barrel as the ale is drawn off, thus ensuring it has a longer life. There is great debate about this system, though. Purists argue (and beer purists always do argue about such matters) that no cask beer should have any gas anywhere near it, however low the pressure and for whatever reason. Personally I never used the system as we sold cask beer extremely quickly because we kept it extremely well, but the matter is for you to decide.

Modern ideas about 'horses' or stillages have taken a lot

of the back-breaking work out of keeping cask beer. Barrels (alas very rarely, nowadays, the proper wooden ones) no longer have to be lifted onto special timber racks well off the floor of cellars. A sloping concrete ramp from the floor itself, about nine inches high, is now thought sufficient. Any man or woman can roll casks easily enough into position on these ramps, chocking them either side so they cannot rock, with a block at the back to be used to tilt the barrel forward as it is emptied. Once again the word 'barrel' may be misleading: you may never order such a thing in your life unless you run a pub with an enormous turnover.

Also on the way out are the marvellously engineered heavy brass taps, being replaced by ugly white plastic ones, to which the beer pipes are attached to the bar pumps. If you do have brass taps, hang onto them. They are now collectors' items. But again, cleanliness. Taps should have boiling water poured over them between use, then a thorough rinsing, to ensure no deleterious deposits of yeast or other muck can contaminate the next barrel.

So how about getting at the beer inside the barrel? Depending on the brewer and the brew it is either very easy or fiendishly tricky and the whole business of 'spiling and tapping' is full of legend.

Let us first make clear what we mean by those words I have been using like cask or barrel. It is unlikely you will ever see a barrel proper, as it holds thirty-six gallons. More common is the kilderkin (or kil) which holds eighteen gallons and is more easily handled. Smaller containers, the nine-gallon firkin or the 4½-gallon pin, can sometimes be found in wood and are often on show behind the bars of pubs which feature 'guest' beers. It is a pleasant throw-back to tradition, especially if you save the old brass taps, as they can be 'drawn from the wood' in the time-honoured fashion, and a very attractive talking-point they make to any bar.

As I mentioned, the barrels are laid on their sides, with the spile hole at the top – a circular disc of wood or plastic with a smaller disc inside it to take the spile – a short, conical-shaped piece of wood to be knocked into the spile hole so that the beer can 'breathe', after it has been allowed to settle.

It all sounds very simple. It can be a very wet-making procedure if you get it wrong. And as with 'tapping' you are often going to get quite wet, before you get the proper knack and can spile and tap a barrel without a single drop being spilled. Once you do manage it, and later do it again successfully, the satisfaction will be immense.

A neat way of spiling a barrel is to use (and make sure it is cleaned thoroughly) a valve from the engine of a car – the piece of turned steel which is in the shape of a T-section. Using a 'soft' mallet (made either of hide or solid rubber), place the smaller end of the valve on the centre of the spile plug and one smart tap will knock the plug into the barrel, which you must then replace by a spile proper. With some beers it is customary to use a 'soft' (that is, slightly porous) spile first, to allow the beer to breathe and then when it is ready to drink replace it with a hard spile. In either case the spiles should be tapped in just hard enough to stop beer frothing out but so that they are easily loosened: they will have to be once you start to draw the beer off, otherwise a vacuum will form inside the cask. The use of the steel valve obviates the problem of using a spile to knock out the spile bung: too hard a wallop and the spile has to be taken out with pliers or, in the worst cases, driven down into the barrel with the danger of breaking the outer seal. But all this depends on what sort of beer you are selling. Only trial and error (sometimes quite a lot of error) will tell you how each beer should be handled.

As an example I always found that draught Bass was without question the 'liveliest' beer of the lot. Even though I made sure it settled for longer than other beers it would still shoot out from the spile hole like an oil 'gusher' before it could be capped with a spile. I always used a clean, thick cloth over the valve when I knocked in the small bung, then held on like grim death while I put in the spile and tapped it gently home to staunch the flow. Before I got the knack with the cloth I could guarantee a fountain of good, sellable Bass would hit the cellar ceiling before I brought it under control. But others beers may be quite docile and give you no trouble.

After a day or so (sometimes, especially with weaker

beers only a few hours) the cask is ready to be 'tapped'. Again it's a knack. Put the conical end of the tap against the bung, make sure it is lined up and – one, two, three, in it goes without a drop being spilled. You are going to get it wrong. You are going to lose a lot of beer in the early days but you will master the act eventually, and a very smart party trick it is. Once I had got the knack I put it to good effect by making sure I had a fullish bar when I tapped one of the guest beers we kept in view of the customers. There was always an appreciative hush and, cross my heart, I never spilled a drop onto the floor. But it still gave me pause for thought as I knew that if I ever got it wrong no one would ever let me forget it.

When a cask is empty, turn off the tap, disconnect the pipe and knock in solid the spile. Turn the cask up on end, loosen the tap by one or two gentle blows to either side and replace it with a bung of the proper size, again knocked in solid. The cask can then be removed to the empties area.

As regards quantities of beer you should keep the brewers' reps will advise you; but in principle you should have one cask in use with another waiting, spiled and tapped, in the case of a busy bar using kils, plus another one 'settling'. A week to ten days' supply is what you should aim for, bearing in mind that breweries deliver once a week. Of course with keg beer there is no settling time, no spiling or tapping in the accepted sense. Just make sure you have sufficient reserves and always at least one spare CO_2 gas cylinder. These are also delivered by the breweries when ordered. Remember, gas cylinders are heavy. They should be stored carefully and never treated casually. It is normal practice to have those in use attached by something like a chain to wall brackets, so that accidental knocks will not result in their falling over and perhaps injuring a foot very badly.

In any event, make sure your cellar is not only clean but that you are fanatically tidy. Crates of beers and soft drinks should be stacked on strong mesh shelves (in themselves easy to clean) and none at a height too great for safety. Easy access is the watchword. Keep such cellar tools as the mallet, pliers, valve, spanners for gas cylinders and beer-pipe connections in a special place and *never* leave them lying about haphazardly. In an ideal storage area – I prefer the term cellar, whether true or not – the floor will be of slightly roughened concrete (to prevent slipping), sloping to a drain grill. It will be equipped with hot and cold water and a large 'Bristol' sink, or a deep stainless steel one. The water taps will be threaded to take hose connections, making everything easy to wash down, and your cleaning fluids, disinfectants, cloths and so on will be stored conveniently safely, along with pressure bottles and pumps, as well as the bags of spiles and bungs which the breweries issue at frequent intervals. Make sure too you have a soap dispenser and hand-towels by the sink. It will be excellently lighted and properly ventilated as well as vermin-proof, including special traps on the main 'artery' which contains the beer pipes between cellar and bar, assuming they are beneath the floors. Remember, mice, or even rats, are quick to find convenient routes around your property and the main pipe conduit between cellar and bars must be kept clear and clean at all times. As a landlord you should never be ashamed of anyone (especially the environmental health officer) taking a look in your cellar. At night, when you close, always go into the cellar to turn off all the taps on the cask beers, tapping in the spiles if you are not using a top low-pressure system. Turn off the gas cylinders that pressurize your keg beers and uncouple and leave loose the connectors. From some of these you may get a dribble of liquor which you should just wash away with clean water, leaving everything fresh and ready for the following morning. If the whole area is kept spotless, and kept so all the time, then I can promise you it will pay dividends in decent beer and other drinks – apart from the fact that it will be much more enjoyable to work in. It is the very engine-room of your pub: do not neglect it.

Wine

Some breweries deal in wines but only a few do so with any knowledge or enthusiasm. Remember, breweries make money from hops, not grapes. They have thereby encouraged whole generations of landlords who actually boast of their ignorance about wine – even today, when that market is increasing at a pace which is the envy of all breweries. On the whole, wines in pubs are poorly chosen, badly served, ludicrously priced and simply not worth drinking. I would like you to be different. I would like you to be a total professional at serving *all* kinds of drinks – and that includes excellent and not overpriced wine, cocktails, even coffee. The modern pub is going to have to change its old 'boozer' image to attract customers in the future. And it has always struck me that professionalism demands a knowledge of all sorts of drinks, not just the traditional, or very alcoholic, ones.

To acquire a reasonable knowledge of wine takes a much longer time, I would suggest, than it does for beer and most spirits. I say 'most' because devotees of malt whisky would argue that their study will take a lifetime and still be incomplete. However, it may be worth your while to keep a small 'wine book' in which you jot down wines you have come across and liked. There is nothing wrong with this – few people can remember details of every wine they have enjoyed, or even disliked. Let us assume that your knowledge of wine is rudimentary but that you are interested in getting a reputation for selling good wine rather than rubbishy plonk: I think there are two courses you can adopt. The first is to make a conscious decision to serve only good, but reasonably priced, wine. And having made such a decision you will go and get some help to that end.

Now of course you may not be interested in the subject at all. You may be buying, or taking the tenancy of, an old spit-and-sawdust beer house where a request for a glass of wine would cause derision tilting towards physical assault. Well, OK. This section is hardly for you – but I have to tell you that such places (and licensees) do still exist and in large numbers. Yet in some ways I do not knock such an attitude: it is at least honest and straightforward. What I do knock is the chap with the wine bottles behind the bar who sells at an inflated price and in the smallest glasses possible the cheapest rubbish he can buy, with an enthusiasm born either of cynicism or ignorance and sometimes, possibly, both.

But putting that aside, you are not going to be like that.

You are going to find a good wine merchant or wholesale drinks supplier which has a rep who specializes in the subject and you are going to listen to the suggestions and buy a few bottles to see if they are suitable. And you are not going to stick stupidly to the 'rule' that there would be six glasses to a bottle. It is not a rule, it is a guideline.

Basically you should stock a decent, 'soft' red, good enough to be drunk on its own without benefit of food. I say this advisedly as some red wines are far too sharp and acidic to stand alone, even among the more expensive bottles. Similarly, go for a dry, but certainly not too acid a white, along with a 'rounder' white wine, but not one which tastes of nothing but sugar and is termed 'sweet' by most licensees. It is unlikely that you will be asked for a *rosé* ordinarily, but a good *rosé* may well be a good seller in hot summer weather. Do not, in any event, ever be tempted by the trick I have personally seen more than once in a bar – the surreptitious mixing in a glass of white and red wines to the required colour. There are a great many ways of ripping off the public, as we shall see, but that really is the bottom line in dishonesty.

Judicious trial of recommended wines – there need be little error if you are taking good advice – will show which wines are popular and which are not. But do try to avoid those 'branded' wines which are produced more and more 'for the trade' and which not only cater for the lowest common denominator of taste but also for a market which, I forecast, will also dwindle, because knowledge never stands still. I reckoned we could sell good wines at a fair price in decent, large glasses when I first came into the business. I was told I was wasting my time. But I was told that by licensees who charged nearly a £1 for less than a four-ounce glass, and I proved them wrong. People used to come to us because they knew that if they wanted a glass or two of wine it would be very good indeed and not cost an arm and a leg. Prices are invidious in any book but just to give you an idea of what I mean a five-ounce (150ml) glass should be the minimum size, and in 1990 a few (alas far too few) pubs I know were selling good wine in a 175ml measure at about £1.20 to £1.65. And I do mean good wine. But in the same year, it must be said, it was common for pubs to sell less than 4ozs of dreadful rotgut for similar prices. However, beware. People are not stupid. They may not complain at the time; they will simply not come back. Establish a good, sound reputation for wine in decent measures at a fair price and your casual customers will become regulars, believe you me. This will allow you to have special, perhaps better, more expensive wines on offer as a feature every week and, at holiday times, even a reasonable champagne on sale by the glass. Impossible in a pub? Nonsense. The name of the game is 'marketing' – but more of that later in the book. Finally, please specify the size of the glass on your price list or display it in the bar. Do be honest with the customer. It really does pay.

There are now cooled wall cabinets available for white wines, if you have the space, but there is nothing wrong with using refrigerated shelves or even the fridge in which to keep white wines at a decent temperature, and by that I mean not too cold. It will probably be some time before your wine turnover demands a special, temperature-controlled cabinet but these are available in sizes which will take fifty or 100 bottles. Red wines, obviously, should be at a warmer temperature but not, as I once saw, kept in a rack above a night-storage heater. It seemed to sum up the average publican's attitude to, and knowledge of wine.

Supplies

Having dealt with beer and cellar matters – both subjects about which you will learn thoroughly on any training course you may attend, with further dollops of knowledge and advice being added every time a brewery rep calls to see you – we should take a look at where you get your supplies.

If yours is a tied house the terms of the tenancy agreement will dictate exactly what you have to buy through the brewery and what can be bought elsewhere. To be fair, there is more latitude for a licensee of a tied house than there used to be, because breweries have for the past few years been forced into corners by EEC regulations, legislation and codes of conduct as well as having to respond to a groundswell of public opinion against them. None of the concessions they made was made willingly, so beware: they will be even more sharp-eyed for the transgressor of any contract.

In any event there will be all sorts of suppliers desperately anxious to get their products on to your shelves. But 'their' product is often misleading. You will be able to buy soft drinks and mixers made by one or the other manufacturer through dozens of suppliers and you will have to make up your mind, especially if you own a free house, just who is going to give you the best deal. So a gentle reminder to listen carefully to the reps.

Now I am going to issue a warning, which first you will doubtless take with a pinch of salt. Once you are started in your new business you are going to remember this paragraph ruefully. The drinks business thrives on paper. You will become inundated with paper. Delivery notes, invoices, demands for payment, changes in prices structures, instructions, urgings to buy this and that, special promotions, revised price lists, notification of single price changes or price increases, credit notes for ullage (returned 'spoiled' beer) or for empty bottles, empty gas cylinders, empty crates. Mountains of paper will pour through your letterbox every day. It will only increase in volume. It will never get less.

So how do you cope with it all?

Well, the way I coped was to find one reliable supplier for all the proprietary mixers, soft drinks, bottled beers, lagers, even some cask and keg beers and lagers and (luckily, in my case) some very good wines. It had two effects. I benefited from the discounts that buying in bulk allowed and instead of paper flooding in from dozens of sources the amount was drastically reduced and therefore more easily understood and handled.

Of course I realize I was lucky to be within the delivery area of a company like Coopers of Wessex, which was reliable, helpful and courteous. You may not be so fortunate but do try to look around carefully. There are many suppliers which are very good indeed and some which are, quite frankly, appalling, offering only poor products and service, whatever they may claim in their brochures or their reps may promise when they call.

Even so you will almost certainly still get your mainstay beers from the breweries themselves, or your 'guest' beers from specialized beer suppliers. All breweries and goods suppliers deliver once a week and their sales staff will telephone you at an agreed time on a certain day each week to receive the orders for the next delivery. Make sure you do not waste your time and theirs on the telephone – have your order written down ready for their call. Most of the people who ring for orders are pleasant and knowledgeable about their products, and for the most part unfailingly cheerful.

You will, however, be subjected to sales pressures not just by the telesales staff but also by the reps. Be careful about this. I mentioned in the last chapter the way in which some customers declare themselves to be regulars but can only drink this or that. Let that be a lesson generally. Do not stock any form of drink that does not 'move'. Be firm about this. We have all seen those dusty bottles of liqueurs on the top shelves of bars, bought probably in good faith for some long-forgotten Christmas. So be choosy about what you stock. Do not stock drinks, especially expensive drinks, just because you 'ought to have them'. You are tying up an awful lot of cash which you could be using in better ways. You should aim for a gross profit margin of at least thirty-five per cent on every drink you sell, but oddly enough you will very rarely lose custom if you do not stock a particular drink, especially if it is a little esoteric. So be sensible and use your judgement and, as you get on, your experience. I can well remember one summer which looked as though it would turn out to be very hot (it was too) and we bought a few bottles of Pimms which we set about 'selling'. We reckoned we could sell anything, given the chance, and a good few cases were shifted before the weather turned autumnal: we were left, incredibly enough, with less than half a bottle, having made a considerable amount of profit in the mean time. We shall consider the whole subject of 'selling' in a later chapter, but never be afraid of either not stocking one particular drink or just buying one bottle 'to see how it will go.'

In this respect a good cash-and-carry will be useful to you. To get a 'card' (that is, become eligible to buy goods) you will have to take your VAT registration document along to the manager, proving that you are a bona fide trade customer, and register your business details, at the same time fixing a credit limit agreeable to you both. It is by no means necessary, however, to buy goods in bulk – that is in dozens or cases of beers, wines or spirits. All wholesalers sell individual items and although few of them could be termed useful to up-market pubs or restaurants they are quite good on basics, not just drink but food, cleaning materials, household goods and kitchenware. None of them is necessarily very much cheaper than your normal suppliers but they do score in drinks like lemonade and some well-known brands of mixers and colas, which they sell by the litre in packs of six or twelve bottles. One possible advantage to you is in the reduction of paperwork. You get one sales note, more often than not itemizing what you bought, and you pay for it there and then. Cash-and-carries make book-keeping very easy.

It may be useful here to mention the modern dispensing methods for mixers and some drinks which are stored in pressurized cylinders. These can be simply 'hosed' into the glass as required from a multi-head, having passed through a cooler. The reps from the drink companies will suggest these to you if your turnover makes them worth while. They save a lot of storage space and labour too – though you may have to keep some bottles (of tonic, cola or soda) for display or emergencies.

And talking of emergencies, the drinks suppliers generally have a 'technical' or service department, as do all the major breweries. They operate a virtually round-the-clock system, so that if anything does go wrong with coolers, pressure systems and so on, they arrive incredibly quickly to deal with the problem. They also call regularly to service or change pieces of equipment.

Drinks Measures

Let me give you a very quick run-down of the regulations as they affect you in your bar: measures for the sale of beers and spirits are strictly laid down by Parliament and enforced by the Weights and Measures Department of HM Customs and Excise as well as the local trading standards officer. These official 'measures' are shortly to be changed to bring them into line with EEC practice and clear warning will be given as to what they are to be and when they are to come into force. This will mean all your dispense 'optics' will have to be changed and the old (and now very valuable) little copper or pewter measuring pots will have gone forever. As a quick guide, at the time of this book going to press, the permitted measures were one-third, one-half or multiples of one-half of a pint for draught beer and cider, which must be dispensed into government-stamped glasses or served from a sealed, stamped cylinder in full view of the customer. Spirits such as whisky, gin, rum, and vodka can only be sold in quantities of a quarter, fifth or sixth of a gill, except in Scotland where one-third is allowed. Wines in carafes must be sold in half- or one-pint quantities or in half, three-quarters or one litre and the measures you are using must be displayed. Wines by the glass are not yet subject to legal stricture, but I have urged you to serve good wines in large glasses and tell the customers what the quantity and the price is. The serving of wines by the glass in Britain has long been a bone of contention and I can confidently forecast that legal regulations will eventually make it precise, quite properly putting to an end the unsavoury practice of serving small glasses at inflated prices.

Draymen
You will also come in contact with delivery drivers or draymen, to use their old name. Only once did I detect any dishonesty in draymen from one particular brewery and I immediately closed the account with them, as I regard such malpractices as emanating from the top – employers should take full responsibility for anything their workforce does.

You will of course hear stories of dishonesty, of the bottom cases of bottled goods, especially beers, being short of a bottle or two, or cases of spirits being one bottle light on being opened. If you are by nature suspicious then obviously make sure all incoming goods are meticulously checked against delivery notes in front of the drayman or van driver. I am afraid I do not have such a nature, and regard all men as honest until proved otherwise, especially draymen who can be very good and useful friends, racking the beers, sorting empties and keeping you in touch with the trade in general.

Such a policy means that once the men know you they can let themselves into your cellar, offload and, in many cases, distribute the delivery and collect all the empties which have been set aside for them. This leaves you free to go out or do something else, although someone will normally have to be on hand to sign the sheets and offer them a drink. You will find that draymen now stick religiously to soft drinks – gone are the days when a pint of best bitter was thought to be the minimum offering from every pub to which they delivered. Not surprisingly, magistrates courts in many cities have records of fines imposed on cheerful draymen being found guilty of being 'drunk in charge of a barrel' in years long past. One can imagine the terror instilled in passers-by who saw a huge wooden barrel (of thirty-six gallons, mind you) rolled inexorably down a street from a dray by hands which were not as steadily controlled as perhaps they should have been.

'Thou Shalt Not'

Finally, for this chapter, a few, very important don'ts. Sadly, all, if not most, of them are disregarded by a great many licensees. Please, please do not become one of the trade's many twisters.

Don't pour slops back into any barrel, whatever the apparent wastage or circumstances. Slops must be thrown away – down the drain. I know you can actually buy long, thin funnels which fit into the spile-hole of a barrel. Do not let me see them in any pub of yours. Murky, smelly, cloudy beer is the inevitable result when the dregs in the sinks beneath the beer pumps are poured back into a casked beer at the end of the evening. The practice became rife in the days when mild ale was very popular, its dark colour hiding the variety of content. But among the unscrupulous the habit dies hard.

Don't keep the heel-taps of mixers like tonic or ginger ale, then pour them back into a bottle at the end of the session and re-cap it with an already used crown top, leaving it 'forward' on the shelf to be sold on to the next (unsuspecting) customer. Heel-taps should go the way of slops – down the drain.

Don't refill empty bottles of good Spanish sherry with British-type sherry and then sell it on at the higher price. And not only with just sherry. The same principle applies whatever the drink.

Don't mix your wines, as in the case of the *rosé* trick above. Dry sherries and similar drinks should not be used to change the taste of sweeter ones, or vice versa.

Don't be too hasty with the optics when customers ask for double measures. I know it's a common trick for barmen to release the second measure before the optic has properly filled from the first, but there is no need for you to do it.

Don't obscure any drink measuring or pouring process from your customer, for example turning your back on him or her while you 'fiddle' with measures or use the optic. Be not only honest but openly honest.

Don't put money or notes into your till before giving the necessary change. Leave whatever the customer has given to you on the shelf above the drawer, in full view of the customer, while you select the change. Having got the right change, put the original money into the drawer slot and shut it. In this way there are fewer disputes about whether he or she gave you a £10 note, say, or a fiver. If in doubt, perhaps because you are not very good at sums (like I am), count the change out for the customer. If you have made a genuine mistake it will stay a genuine mistake and not give rise to suspicions. Short changing (as well as short measures) is a common practice, especially in busy bars. If you allow suspicions to arise you will never get rid of them in people's minds.

Don't put your thumb over the rim of a tankard, or any other glass, or even into it, when drawing beers. It is a common habit and a dirty one. Hold the glass by the handle or round it near the bottom, if it is what is called a 'sleever'.

Don't stick the top of the bottle into the glass, and never into the liquor, when pouring drinks like bottled beers. Again it is a filthy habit.

Finally: DON'T CHEAT THE PUBLIC – EVER.

7 Catering for Your Customers

It is widely assumed that if you have a pub then you must do food. Not at all. I know some landlords who do no food at all – not because they are too lazy or stupid, but simply because they have made a rational decision suited to their own circumstances.

Serving food can cause all sorts of problems and headaches. Think carefully before you embark on an idea which you may regret. On the other hand you may justifiably feel that you would like a share of the estimated £12 billion which customers spend on eating in pubs every year.

Pub Grub

The serving of food in pubs is a very recent phenomenon. It may seem strange but not so many years ago the idea of finding anything to eat in a pub other than a bag of potato crisps or a packet of peanuts, was so rare as to excite disbelief. I suppose the first step was bread and cheese and, indeed, the road downhill to the awful 'pub grub' of today began with that frightful word 'Ploughman's'. I do hope that whoever coined the word has long ago been led away and shot.

It is true, but only to a certain extent, that the provision of food can make the difference between profit and loss for many pubs. But people who support this idea never say what sort of food will make the difference. And in this respect you must carry out quite a lot of your own market research. And having done so, decide very deliberately what you are going to do and how you are going to do it. Do not confuse your own, perhaps small, pub offering a limited choice of 'homely' dishes with such huge chains of eateries as Berni Inn or Beefeater. In fact, these can no longer be classed as pubs doing food, but are in effect full-blown, fully licensed restaurants. We shall consider in Chapter 13 how a move from humble pub to inn/ restaurant may eventually be accomplished but do not run before you have even started to toddle.

As you may already have guessed I am not particularly fond of 'pub grub'. I am not one of those people who believe the food you find in pubs is cheaper and better than you can find anywhere else. It is frequently cheap, yes, because what has gone into it was cheap – and very often nasty. It also benefits from being served in a building the overheads of which are meant to be paid for by the sale of booze.

Financial Factors

From the money point of view you should aim for a gross profit margin of roughly sixty-five per cent on any food you serve. I say 'aim' because such a margin may well be too much in some cases, and too little in others. Use the figure as a guide, and watch what other people charge in places similar to yours – but do not make the mistake of forgetting that quality must be part of any equation. I advise you to serve the best-quality produce you can get hold of – and that applies to all ingredients, whether it be meat, fish, vegetables, cheeses, eggs and cream. Do not use substitutes. Do not believe the blandishments of the advertisers, who urge you to use this or that substitute, which is 'just like the real thing'. It is not and will never be.

However, you may decide not to do food: it may cause more problems than you can manage; you do not have a suitable kitchen or it will be too expensive to bring up to Environmental Health standards (now getting tougher all the time); you will need staff which you cannot get or do not want; there are more than enough places in your immediate area already doing it – and much better than you can; you have no lunch trade to warrant food at that time, and in the evening your clientele is not the sort who would want it.

Added to this there are some basic considerations of

accountancy. Looking first on the gloomy side can be dispiriting, I quite realise, but I just want to put pub food into perspective from the outset.

Most pubs rely on the landlord's wife to do the cooking. And very few landlords ever bother to cost out that facility in real terms. You really must not ignore either yourself or your wife in such considerations. To regard a key staff member as 'free' is no way to run a business. The moment you add in wages for the landlord's wife (at a cost equivalent to a full-time cook) then a very different picture often emerges. And that is not all, alas. Let us take a closer look at real profits on one item on a menu, as revealed in a business survey in the *Caterer and Hotelkeeper*.

Most pubs seem obliged to offer steak-and-kidney pie and two vegetables to the public. In 1990 the average price charged by licensed premises was £2.80.

Food cost	1.15
Gross profit (46%)	1.29
	2.44
VAT	.36
Selling price	£2.80

To get a gross profit of sixty per cent the selling price of the dish would have to be at least £4.20 and for a 70% gross profit it would have to be sold at £7.

Continuing the example take a look at your labour costs:

Cook	4.50 per hour
Server	3.00
Other help	2.60
Total	£10.10 per hour.

Assuming staff are on duty three hours at lunchtime, your labour costs stand at £30.30. So with only £1.29 profit on your steak-and-kidney pie you will need to serve twenty-four diners simply to break even. That is a lot of people. Very few small pubs can achieve this customer turnover and if you are serving things like steak or the ubiquitous Ploughman's your profit margin will be even less.

But, I can hear people say, by serving food we can

increase our bar sales dramatically. 'Dramatic' would be the right word if you were certain that the increased profits on the wet sales more than offset losses on the food. Such certainty would be against the trend, which sadly shows that very few pubs actually do break even on food.

So, why do so many pubs go on with the notion if it is such a stupid idea? Well, few landlords have done such accountant's sums. If they were accountants they would not be publicans, and most publicans regard their whole way of life as more important to them and their customers than any set of figures. Which means that wives (or husbands, for that matter) will still slave over a hot stove, even though it could well be a slippery slope into bankruptcy.

However, on a brighter note, just bear in mind that I am writing this chapter about serving food, not about not serving it and there may be many reasons why you should consider serving *some* food, whether it is a cheese roll or soup and some bread. Too much of the world and its wonders is now controlled by accountants, often to the detriment of ordinary men and women to whom the word 'service' means more than the word 'profit'. The decision will be yours alone, but give it a chance – ensure it could be worth your while by doing a lot of local research, as I said before. You must go round all the pubs in your area and see what they are serving, and at what price. You may find, quite to your surprise, that there is a very definite niche you could fill and it may persuade you to try your hand at it.

Why Is Pub Food So Dreadful?

I have to say that the (possibly oversimplified) answer to this is the fact that cooking in Britain is still considered beneath serious thought, and from this springs a number of other prejudices: that it is not considered a proper skill; that any old fool can cook; that if you can cook an omelette for the family you can cook huge dinners for vast numbers of people; that cooking isn't needed nowadays (you can buy everything in and pop it into boiling water – even your salads come out of a bucket); the average punter can't tell chalk from cheese, let alone margarine from butter, doesn't care anyway and even if he did he wouldn't complain because that is not 'the British' thing to do.

Now at first sight, and, alas, to a great number of people in the catering business, all the above statements are true. But are they? I shall surprise you. The last statement is quite definitely not true. What may be true is that the British do not complain but what is not true is that the British public do not know or care about decent food. If you make that assumption you do so at your peril. What is certainly true is that if you serve mediocre food, as most pubs (and even a great many restaurants) do, you will get mediocre people, and because everything is mediocre it will not matter to them if they keep on coming or go somewhere else. People who like good food – and they are the people who are important eventually, whose numbers increase each year – will only come to your pub once. They will avoid it after that. So what do you do? You serve excellent food. You serve better food than any of your competitors.

But the food you serve must be within your capabilities, knowledge and experience.

In one book I have read about running a pub the author states that there is nothing mysterious about cooking. It is a curious adjective to use, but if by that he meant it is an unskilled, easy task then he is merely endorsing the remarks I made above. It is precisely because of this attitude that pub food is so frightful. If you cannot cook, then go and learn about it or get someone in to do it for you. Do not, as many people do, simply go to the nearest cash-and-carry and buy in all those sealed trays and cans of institutional food which you just heat up and claim is 'home cooked'.

Indeed, the words 'home cooked' always make me shudder. I think we must be the only country in the world with a need to make that claim. What a reflection on us as a nation. And how sad that it should be necessary.

So, once again, let us consider what *is* within your capability. Well, how about a sandwich? But your idea of a sandwich may be different from mine. I suppose that does not matter providing you more than fulfil your customer's idea of a sandwich. Alas, very few pubs do.

Some years back I used to go to a pub on a main road just

outside the Sussex town of Midhurst. It was a pleasant enough place with a cheerful staff even though often under extreme pressure. On the bar there was a glass display cabinet. In that cabinet was a small selection of sandwiches – but they were so vast, so tempting, so overflowing with goodness that strong men drooled over them while waiting for their pints. The prawns, in a properly made mayonnaise, fell out of the bread on all sides, the beef, red, rare and thinly sliced, was piled up layer on layer; cheese and tomato and cucumber and fresh lettuce cried out profligately to be eaten. Making a choice, any choice, was an agony of indecision. I used to plan journeys which allowed me to stop at that pub for one of their sandwiches at lunchtime. So did a great number of other customers. But the inevitable happened. One day I stopped there and knew at once it had changed hands. The place had been 'tarted up'. Gone was the crush of customers – and gone was the display cabinet. In its place was one of those terrible thick plastic menu covers got up to look like real hide. My humble request for a sandwich was met with disdain and offhandedness. What sort did I want? I left my half pint on the counter and have never been back.

Now the moral of that story is simple. If you are going to do a sandwich, do a proper one. And do not be afraid to charge a fair and decent price for it; customers will happily pay good money for good things. And if you do not know what a real sandwich is, go and find out. A sandwich is not two slices of thick bread, spread with an oily smudge of veggie-grease, between which is placed a so called slice of reconstituted, rubbery tasteless ham that owes more to a surgeon's skill in slicing membrane thinly than it does to a bread knife. The definition of a sandwich in a famous Danish book on the subject actually feels the need to state in its British edition that the most important part of any sandwich is the generosity of its filling and the skill with which it has been put together. It is a sad reflection on what that Danish author thinks of Britain's attitudes towards one of his great national passions. And I would draw your attention to the use of the word 'filling'. He did not mean 'garnish' – that totally useless and inappropriate collection of onion ring, bit of tomato, slice of cucumber and some cress on the side of the plate. That has nothing to do with a real sandwich, any more than an old bap containing a thin slice of processed plastic has to do with a cheese roll. Yes, make sure even your humblest food appeals to the eye as well as the palate, but please do not try to hoodwink your customer, as a great many publicans do, by covering up their financial greed or lack of expertise with a load of old 'garnish', which does nothing for the palate and is tiresome to eat anyway.

So I hope that even if your sights are set on what you and others might call 'just a sandwich', when a customer asks if you have anything to eat, just make sure that *your* sandwich is by far away the very best served in the entire area. In that way your reputation for excellence will spread, and spread deservedly and quickly.

Now it so happens that I deliberately chose the so-called 'humble' sandwich as an example of the problems of providing food in your pub. In fact, a (proper) sandwich is, as they say, very 'labour intensive' and many pubs actually avoid serving them because it can gum up what may be a busy kitchen for quite some time. This could well be the reason why so many sandwiches are so dreadful: a cheap and nasty offering of the sort you normally get takes no time at all, whereas a real humdinger is an act of inspired creation – and time. But it also illustrates what your approach should be towards the provision of food generally: a determination to provide only the best, whatever the food; a finely judged choice (if choice there be) which is within your capabilities – thereby avoiding any temptation to offer what is horrendously called 'an extensive menu' (that is, convenience or junk food from the freezer); care in the planning, preparation and service of all food; and, finally, the courage to say 'no' to a customer, either because you have run out of what he wishes to order or just because you are not able to do it properly. It is better to disappoint a customer by not serving him food than to serve him disappointing food for which he is expected to pay.

Planning

There is one very important word which I used in the

above paragraph: 'planning'. This is the key to success or failure. Plan, minutely, what food you are going to serve and how. If, for instance, you are to specialize in sandwiches, make sure all your ingredients are set out in bowls on the table in plenty of time, not just set out, of course, but with the fillings ready to use. Make sure you have decent bread sliced and waiting (covered, like the other ingredients, when not in use) and good butter at a spreadable consistency. Remember that you can sell food by its appearance, just as that pub did near Midhurst. So always make sure that, as far as possible, what you are offering is 'on show' while people get their drinks. A large, beautifully arranged and generously filled chill-cabinet may not be within your orbit to start with, but you can still contrive to put on display a small selection of sandwiches, say, on a clingfilm covered tray which will be sufficiently tempting. And small purpose-made plastic display cabinets are easily and cheaply available from specialist catering and licensed trade outlets.

Now although a great many writers and advisers are always pressing for 'local' and 'fresh' produce to be used in pubs, the pressure of other work, or ignorance about cooking or running a kitchen, can often mean instead the tired, old sameness of the bought-in or frozen product. It is this lack of imagination which results in pubs from Penzance to Perth coming up with the same menus. If one day a major manufacturer puts on to the market a ready-to-use, portion-controlled pack of, say, mushrooms in garlic breadcrumbs, then ten-to-one that very same product will appear on every one of a dozen pub menus in every town throughout the land – and all within a matter of a month or so. I find it acutely depressing, but if you are going to run your pub as a special place, food can be your great opportunity to cash in with something quite different. Simplicity and excellence is the keynote. But a word in your ear: you do not have to make everything yourself; nor do you have to use exclusively a huge wholesaler or cash-and-carry. You should go out and find a good local baker to supply you with fresh bread and rolls; find local growers for vegetables and fruit for your kitchen, flowers for your tables; and are there no local 'cooks' who are a dab hand at pies; puddings, chutneys, jams and so on, who would be more than willing to sell their expertise to you?

I realize, of course, that if you have a pub in a large city some of this advice may seem rather stupid. But very few newcomers to the trade actually do take those sort of pubs. Most take them in country towns or the country itself – and yet still persist in buying those frightful commercial products you can see on all supermarket shelves. Why? Lack of imagination, that is why. Let me give you an example which many of you may well be able to follow.

Most country towns and villages in Britain have a local 'WI' – or Women's Institute. And most have a 'market' once a week where their goods are sold to the general public. What a wondrous Aladdin's cave of goodies is available there for you. Pots of home-made jams, pickles, chutneys. Fresh butter, cream, cheese and eggs. Cakes, pies, tarts, quiches. All manner of vegetables, flowers and plants. And all, generally of unsurpassable quality ... The idea of your going to the local WI market may well raise a smile. I wonder why. It may well be because attitudes to good food are so curious in this country, especially good food in the one place where you should be able to find it, but so rarely do – the local pub. Do not be too quick to scoff. Try it, as I did. I had as much as I could made by own local WI. Fresh horseradish cream was delivered on Sunday mornings to go with the joint of roast ribs of beef for lunch; all our flowers were supplied (and often arranged) by helpers from the WI and all week I had offers of the very best produce from gardens. It all came about because I made it known that we were 'in the market' for anything that was good, fresh and of superb quality. It is true that we had a large garden ourselves which supplied the kitchen with all manner of good things, but never enough for our needs. I found the local WI enjoyed helping us out – and our customers recognized the quality when they ate it.

Perhaps you may not be as lucky as I have been with suppliers. But even so there is no need at all, in my opinion, to resort to what other licensees do and just copy what everyone else does, albeit often rather poorly. Keep an eye open for specialist suppliers in your neighbourhood. I was lucky to be able to use an excellent local firm which provided marvellous fish, shellfish and game. I also found, as you should do, a very good retail butcher who provided me with excellent meat, and at a discount. The surprising thing about my mentioning all this is that I should need to at all. Alas, there is. Few licensees provide good, fresh food. In fact the widespread popularity of the freezer and the bulk-catering company has done more to damage the cause of decent food in Britain than any other factor. It has just made everything too easy. Why go to the trouble, so many people argue, of cooking anything yourself when someone 'out there' has done it all for you? I just hope you are not one of them.

'Menuese'

The widespread use of dull, 'bought-in' foods has also led to the widespread use of that appalling, pretentious 'menu speak', which most customers find hilariously funny, but which is taken as a serious sales point by the average publican. Phrases like 'tangy lemon wedge', 'dew-fresh', 'morning-picked', *'real* cream'; words like 'tasty', 'crusty', 'fresh' imply to me that none of the offerings are anything of the sort. After all, everything should be like that – descriptions should be superfluous. Alas, the British alone in Europe feel the need for such silliness – largely because their food is so poor. And saddest of all: the dear, dreary 'home-made'. You see, I believe honestly that your food should actually and truly be all of these things and should not need pathetic adjectives to give them a spurious boost. If you drop the hyperbole and instead concentrate on turning the best ingredients into the best dishes you will never go far wrong, however 'simple' (and therefore, to me, attractive) your menu is. And as a bonus, your customers will like it too, and tell other people.

Now I do realize that whatever I say many licensees will still regard 'menu speak' as essential for attracting customers to eat at all. So be it. But I do not, and I honestly believe that it puts off a great many people. As a final, but true, example of all that I loathe I quote from a ludicrous

Christmas menu sent to me by the very successful landlord of The Griffin at Fletching in Sussex. Let me hasten to say it was not his menu, but one of his competitors. Among a 'range' of dishes it included (and I quote verbatim):

Festive Soup of the Day

*

Santa's Delicously Refreshing Melon,
drenched in Kirsch

*

Roasted Sussex Turkey,
served with a Bacon and Sausage Roulade,
accompanied by a steaming Yule Tide Cranberry Sauce

*

Colonial Goose from Down Under

*

Christmas Plum Pudding, garnished with holly

If you think that funny then you will have understood my message. If you think it is a great menu and unfaultable then you will be joining a great army of landlords who think likewise, and good luck to you all.

While on the subject of Christmas I would like to encourage you to be a little different whenever you can, and not slavishly follow what everyone else is doing. I remember some time back that we made a vow never to put turkey on the menu around Christmas. We actually made capital out of it too – by making sure everyone in our area knew that no turkey would ever cross our threshold, dead or alive. Our business increased just because of this novelty factor. And it drew from one of our brewery reps a sigh of relief as he looked at the menu before sitting down with one of his business colleagues whom he was entertaining. He remarked that everywhere he went he was made to eat turkey. So much so that when Christmas came round he could not face sitting down to yet more turkey with his own family, so he had something like a pork chop.

With or Without Chips?

This chapter is meant to be about serving food in a pub, yet I seem to be riding hobby horses of my own, pleading with you not to do certain things instead of advising you what to do. Yes, you are right. And here is another 'don't'. Don't serve chips unless you have proper kitchen extraction equipment. Unless, of course, you want your whole pub to smell as evil as every other pub does. Nothing, but nothing, is worse than the smell of stale cooking oil and chips. It clings to everyone's clothes and hair. It swamps all the good things a good pub should smell of – cleanliness, polish, bright fragrant beer, the welcoming scents of good, wholesome cooking. It surrounds you the moment you stop your car, follows you when you leave, and will cloak your staff and clog your furnishings.

What, I hear you say, no chips at all? That is exactly what I say. I have never served chips, not because I do not like them but because I have never managed to afford a good enough extraction or air-cleaning system. And let me add that if you too do not serve chips it will make not one jot of difference to your takings. Indeed, your customers might even comment favourably just because there is no smell, tell their friends about their 'find' and actually increase your turnover.

I shall reinforce what to many will seem an extraordinary statement by giving as a true example a decision made by friends of ours who run a very success-ful pub in Dorset. For some time they appeared as regular customers, once a week, to eat lunch in our bar and they eventually asked why we never served chips. We told them the reason and they then 'owned up' that they too were licensees, who came to eat with us rather than in the main town where they regularly shopped. After listening to us they decided never to serve chips again as they too were conscious of the smell, however often they cleaned the fryer or changed the oil. To this day there are no chips served in that pub. Yet it is packed out and you often have to book a table a week or more ahead to make sure you get fed. As a rider, and again because of our humble example, they also started to 'phase out' the ubiquitous Ploughman's. That too made no difference to their turnover and most customers never noticed its passing.

The Environmental Health Officer

Later on in this book we shall come across the formidable and increasing bureaucracy which will affect all your working life. You will certainly learn the hard way that whatever governments and politicians say about improving the lot of the self-employed, the small business man or woman, they mean no such thing. You are easier to 'get at' than the big conglomerates and the complexity of your life will increase accordingly. This is particularly true when it comes to serving food to the public for it is in this sphere that the Environmental Health Officer (EHO) reigns (or would like to) supreme.

Now I accept, as most reasonable people would, that you have no wish to poison the people who come to eat your food. In the first place it is unkind and in the second place it is distinctly counter-productive. The EHO thinks no such thing. He sees the world of public catering as one vast and sinister plot to infect humble souls with the most fiendish and terrible poisons. As a body of people they have manipulated the public media to great effect, blowing up out of all proportion the number of genuine cases of food poisoning each year (most of which are contracted as a result of home cooking or, inevitably, institutional food made on a massive scale), so that it is difficult to determine the truth from the exaggeration. However, they make their impact on the public mind by their 'watchdog' powers over smaller caterers. If you intend to serve food, therefore, you would do well to ask your local EHO to call by to discuss your plans and to seek his advice on how best to comply with the regulations. Bear in mind, however, that some 'regulations' may be of his own mental fantasy. If in doubt you may well have to ask to see the actual legal paragraphs – but not yet. It is better if, at the start, you set off in the manner you hope will be appreciated: as a supplicant seeking his help and advice, attentive to his every word.

I have, naturally, been particularly cynical about the EHO. I hope you will not come to see this for yourself but you must be warned that power corrupts and it takes a strong man to resist it. Many years ago the EHOs were men of considerable experience and of an almost world-weary disposition. Most were comfortingly middle-aged and had no wish to cause waves when small ripples would suffice. Their help and advice could be sought without fear. They made suggestions rather than demands. They bent over backwards to understand your problems, often bending the rules a little because they were able to recognize that some problems were insurmountable. The important thing, as a caterer, was that you tried. You tried to do as much as was humanly possible to ensure the public was protected. If you did that, genuinely and honestly, you earned nothing but a pat on the back from the EHO. But times have changed. The older men have been replaced by eager hounds, anxious to make their mark with their paymasters and no longer content to regard their job as preventive. Prevention may be better than cure but not, most modern EHOs argue, unless it is seen to be done in the full blaze of aggressive publicity. The result has been unfortunate for a great many 'small' caterers, because the demands made of them have all too often proved impossible to fulfil, with the best will in the world.

So you must bear all this in mind when you first ask to see him. If he is fair he will also be helpful and aware of the problems you may have. He will understand, for instance, that money will almost certainly be tight; that the demands on your purse-strings will be manifold; that a great many of those demands will be priorities. If you are lucky, he will set a rough and ready sort of timescale, a date to aim for, rather than an unmovable deadline, for any alterations or improvements he suggests. And he will certainly suggest something, believe you me.

Under normal circumstances the EHO will inspect those areas of concern to him – that is, kitchen, food storage areas and their surroundings, dining areas and the bar (over which he also has jurisdiction), the toilets and your cellar or where your beers and other drinks are kept, and draw up a comprehensive, written report for you. The service is, of course, free. Please do not be tempted into serving food without telling the EHO first and then asking for a visit. Even if you are taking over a pub which has been serving food, either ask the outgoing landlord if he has a recent report from the EHO or, if not, ask the EHO to call as soon as he finds it convenient.

Once you have the report you can discuss with the EHO what are the priorities as he sees them and what sort of time-scale will be involved. It is important to understand that if you serve food to the public you have to comply with some basic requirements, otherwise the EHO can make application to the magistrates court for a closure order against you. As this book is being written the EHOs are pressing the Government to make it obligatory for all caterers (whatever their size or type) to be licensed, exactly in the same way as any publican has to be in order to sell alcohol. I can forecast success in their campaign – bear in mind what I said about increasing bureaucracy. But it may be helpful here to give you a very brief idea of the sort of things he will be looking for and what he may demand. For the most part it is plain common sense.

Cleanliness is the first thing. In this the EHO (as in so many other things) regards himself as God. He will act as though he alone knows what cleanliness is, as though it were he who discovered it. Your kitchen and food areas must not only be clean, they must appear to be virtually self-cleaning. He will demand that there are no nooks and crannies which can 'harbour dirt' (a favourite phrase of his), that all walls, ceilings and floors are as antiseptic as an operating theatre, but a lot more easily kept that way. You will have to have a hand-basin and a 'drying facility' so that you and your staff can wash hands every second of the day, ignoring the other two sinks you will also require – one for washing-up and the other for vegetables and so on. (After all, no one, but no one has ever washed their hands in the kitchen sink, have they?) All EHOs have a fetish about washing hands, walls, ceilings, floors, pots, pans, ovens and shelves. It is understandable because these are inanimate objects and inanimate objects can attract legislation. It is different with people. EHOs will not grasp the simple fact that you can have a whole kitchen so clean that everything will taste and smell of antiseptic, and yet customers can still get food poisoning because some filthy, uncaring member of staff is simply filthy and uncaring and impossible to legislate against. But even this may change: yet another regulation heading for the statute book is aimed at a licensing system for food handlers in all catering establishments.

The EHO will also want to see food storage areas which should not only be spotlessly clean and easily cleanable but also well ventilated, with the lower shelf at least eight inches above the floor. All doors must be vermin-proof. Similar requirements will also apply to your cellar and where you store drinks.

In the bar he will inspect the cleanliness of all shelving, flooring and so on, see whether you have hand-washing and drying equipment, and almost certainly suggest alterations to bring it 'into line with modern practices'. This is almost impossible to achieve in reality, as are many of the EHO's strictures, for you have to remember that he knows absolutely nothing of what it means to work in such places, nor does he have any interest in the idea.

Of course, even if you do not serve food the EHO still has to advise about bars, cellars and toilets, but I have brought all these questions together in this chapter to give you an idea of the extent of his jurisdiction. It may be fair to say that he will be a little less interested in your pub if you do not serve any form of food or, if that is unkind, he will tend to call on you for 'spot checks' less often.

You may remember my use of the word 'cynical' earlier in this section. You will also notice that I have kept up the theme. I have done it deliberately, just to warn you. I have tried to paint as black a picture of the EHO as I can in the hope that you will find him far less demanding and unreasonable than I have made him sound. With any luck you will find him courteous, helpful and understanding –

as I have done with a number throughout the years. But you may also find a character who is just the opposite, a pain in the neck. I have tried to warn you. I do hope fortune smiles on you.

Kitchen Equipment
As regards the equipment you will need in the kitchen, this again depends entirely on the sort of food you are going to do and the numbers of people you expect to serve.

If you are taking over a pub already in the food business and intend to continue in that way, I suggest most strongly that you do absolutely nothing by way of alterations, buying new equipment and so on until you have established exactly what you will need. The previous licensee may have rubbed along pretty well on what he had but most kitchens are badly laid out. Few kitchens in pubs (or anywhere else) have ever been designed by a chef. Most of the time they have got that way by odd bits of equipment being shoved in here and there just because they fitted at that time. But no matter, if it works for someone else it may work for you, so alter nothing until you are absolutely certain you know what you want.

But supposing your new pub has never done food, what then? Well, for a start you may be able to soldier on without great expense by using what you already have. Take no great notice of those experts who will tell you that ordinary domestic equipment is no good in a commercial kitchen. They are wrong. Some domestic equipment does very well in the kitchens of small pubs, providing the demand is no greater than that of a reasonable family. So, once again, decide what sort of food you are going to do and stick to that decision. Do not set your sights too high at the start. Begin humbly and as your experience improves, along with your market research into what is needed, then you can possibly increase your range too. By that time you will have a better idea of what sort of equipment you will need.

In the first place, of course, you will need a cooker. The problem with most domestic cookers is that their tops are simply not big enough for the rather larger saucepans you may have to use. OK, you may get one large pot on the top, but when you add a frying-pan there is little room left for anything else. Most newcomers seem to concentrate on oven sizes – actually not at all unreasonable in most domestic cookers – but what is professionally known as the 'boiling table' really does need to be a lot bigger than the standard domestic 22-inch square, four-ring cooker top and with rather more powerful burners.

Ideally, I would urge you to forget the idea of the conventional cooker with rings on top and ovens underneath. In a professional kitchen such an arrangement is far from ideal. It is better to have a boiling table with at least six rings and storage racks underneath and then ovens, also at work-top height, adjacent or in another area. All chefs, of course, have their own preferences but mine is for gas rings (burners) and electric ovens. This to me is the best of both worlds. And a final word on ovens: if you have space or need for only one oven take care about selecting one which is fan-assisted. They are marvellous pieces of equipment – but only for certain things. Take a simple example. Bread and foods like Yorkshire pudding cook excellently and much more quickly in fan-assisted ovens. On the other hand, put in something which needs slow and gentle cooking, perhaps without a lid, and within minutes the moisture has gone and the food has dried out. By all means have a small fan-assisted oven but do make sure you have a conventional one as well.

Of course, as in most things today, manufacturers are now producing ovens which combine all sorts of functions – microwave, fan-assisted, convection, even steam, all rolled into one. Expensive, undoubtedly, and they can seem attractive to certain operations but not, I would suggest, to yours. Stick to basics and do think carefully before rushing out to buy a microwave. Reliance on a microwave oven has ruined more food and pub reputations than it has ever made. You may not agree with me that they are inventions of the devil and best left severely alone until you have learned how to operate your kitchen properly but at the very least please take heed of the many dire safety warnings which have been issued about using domestic microwave ovens in commercial kitchens. They rarely last long enough to make them cost efficient and they can well be short of essential radiation protection. Many cooks regard microwave ovens, quite properly in my opinion, as nothing more useful than a cooking tool, like a food processor or a set of excellent knives. A microwave is not a primary cooking tool – it is merely, and only in experienced hands, a useful adjunct to a busy kitchen.

Apart from the actual cooking equipment like a boiling table and an oven you will need at least two sinks (one for vegetables, the other for pots and pans etc) and, to satisfy the Environmental Health Officer, a separate basin for washing hands. Your work-tops should be adequate in size and number for what you intend, easily cleaned and preferably stainless steel. You will also need shelving, again cleanable and lots of it. Do try to avoid storing utensils in cupboards – the curse of the domestic 'fitted' kitchen. All cupboards have doors and busy cooks always have at least one hand full of something hot when something else is needed from behind that door. Cupboard doors are at best exasperating and at worst dangerous if they project over walkways or above work surfaces. Keep your cupboards for things like dry goods, packaged foods and so on. Pots and pans, cooking utensils and cutlery are best kept on handy shelving, on wall fitments or hanging from convenient hooks.

Some of your kitchen equipment may be bought second hand but I would urge you first and foremost to visit the showroom of a good catering supplier, and preferably more than one. You will find them in Yellow Pages under 'Catering Equipment' and you may be lucky to have quite a number more or less local to your new pub. It matters not whether you intend to buy anything at that moment but it allows you to find out, inspect and discuss the merits of what is on the market and the sort of prices you will be expected to pay. Also do try to go to the big national (or regional) catering exhibitions. The sales assistants at the showrooms and at the exhibitions are a fount of knowledge and for the most part offer excellent, courteous advice and help. The first thing that may surprise you, is how the manufacturers seem to have 'thought of everything'. You will soon come to recognize the names of the leading manufactuers of catering equipment, virtually all of whom now supply a complete range of modular units which can be literally added on as required to a basic cooking unit such as a boiling table or oven. You will also find such remarkable inventions as broiler plates which make the frying-pan a thing of the past.

But – and it is a big BUT – before you plunge into anything, second-hand or new, take very careful stock of whether you truly want a deep fryer. And if you do, observe a few simple rules: (1) Make sure that the necessary fume extraction and/or air cleaning equipment has been installed, or can be, quickly and easily, before you actually use the fryer. You surely do not want to smell as foul as most of your competitors do? (2) Make sure the fryer has what is technically called a secondary high-limit thermostat which cuts off the fuel supply instantly if the main thermostat fails and the cooking oil rises to 575 degrees Fahrenheit or above. A great many serious fires are caused by oil overheating beyond its flash-point because of a faulty primary thermostat. (3) Make sure the fryer 'element' (whether electricity or gas) is powerful enough for your expected demand. Too low a heating or 'recovery' ability means food gets soggy while your cook becomes exasperated waiting for food to be cooked. All fryers should conform to British Standard specification BS5784 which deals with their efficiency in this respect. (4) Make sure your new fryer has either a built-in, pump-based oil filtration unit or a simple system by which oil can be cleaned and re-used or completely emptied, cleanly and without fuss, once the oil-life is finished. (5) Make sure you have costed a fryer correctly, and not just considered the capital cost, as energy consumption and oil usage adds significantly to kitchen expenses.

But however well your kitchen is equipped, it is the food it produces that matters more than anything else. The most marvellous equipment can still produce the most appalling food, whereas good cooks can conjure up marvels from a single ring and a biscuit-tin oven.

Regional Cooking

Finally I want to end this chapter with a few words from an article I was asked to write for the *Morning Advertiser* some time ago.

In a country as small as Britain is there, can there ever be, such a thing as 'regional' cooking? And even if there was such a thing, and easy recipes made it possible, would it be any use – especially when all a pub customer ever wants is steak-and-kidney pie?

Oh dear, steak-and-kidney pie *again*? Yes, I am afraid so – that monstrous tribute to lack of culinary imagination, expertise and skill – all beckoning like crones from menu-boards in every high-street, on every village green. Recently I was in Chichester. I swear that no fewer than five pubs actually brandished this dish under the noses of passers-by – and they were *proud* of it. Dammit, the temperature was just under 90 degrees Fahrenheit.

But let's start gently (forget the good summer, autumn's nigh); Lancashire Hotpot, Irish Stew. Good, good. Everyone's heard of them, though few ever cook it. Then there's Cornish Pasties (nobody seems to make those anymore, just relying on a central supplier for a foul and peppery concoction only suitable for grockles. And the Devon Pastie has been quite forgotten). Haggis, Colcannon and Pan Haggerty – yes, of course. Next, perhaps, Somerset Casserole, Sussex Brawn, even Sussex Pond Pudding, Cornish Charter Pie, Cheese Wundy, Cotswold Dumplings. And how many pubs in Wales serve Tarts Sioned, Swper Sgadan? In the Isle of Man, Herring Pie? In Yorkshire, Old Wives Sod? And in Scotland where are the mealies, white pudding or Tuppenny Struggles? Still uncertain about regional food? Nonsense. That's only a tiny start.

Alas, in those very places where something local would be really apt – the pub – you never find anything local at all. Regional cooking, regional dishes, regional produce – what's that, you all say? The steak and kidney is easier, it comes out of a bucket, a tin, a foil-pack, all centrally manufactured and supplied and all tasting exactly the same – dreadful. Thus a felony is compounded. In the first instance no pub offers regional food, and in the second they offer food which looks, tastes and *is* exactly the same wherever you go. A further crime is committed by saying it is what people want. Utter balderdash. Customers eat it because it is the only thing offered, because it has sunk to such an abysmal level of brown tastelessness that it is 'safer' than anything else. But junk the junk and just try something different and see what happens. Go to the library. Borrow the regional 'taste of ...' book, published by your local Tourist Board. It may be a load of hype, it may not be very accurate, but at least it's a start in the right direction.

Mind you, southerners are the worst culprits. Thank God in parts of Yorkshire, especially Bradford, Bingley and Haworth (home of the Brontës – Britain's number two for literary shrines) you can still buy that memorable bar snack, a whacking circle of crisp-edged, freshly cooked Yorkshire pudding along with its attendant jug of meaty onion gravy. And they still serve mushy peas – no, not as a veg., but a bar snack in a bowl, with a jug of mint sauce to go with it – a favourite among German businessmen visiting local factories. In Lancashire, thickly cut black pudding (from Bury, of course) with bread-and-butter is back on some bar menus – and it will not be long before tripe-and-onions, or even cold, honey-comb tripe with vinegar returns to general fashion.

Bit too strong for effete southern stomachs, eh? Well, I speak of regional food, not mass-produced answers to culinary boredom and crass ignorance. Would even one local, regional dish be too daring, too presumptuous?

But be warned. I do not want to find haggis on every pub menu. I do not want Yorkshire pudding and onion gravy in every London pub (and thank God we are not offered it – the mind boggles as to what it might look like) and I do not even want

Crempog Las beyond Fishguard, Exmoor Toasts beyond Doone country, chudlies and clotted cream beyond Devon. But I wouldn't mind something good and local, well cooked and interesting, delicious and different, something just to try for the first time. Am I asking too much, for goodness' sake? And can I make one more plea? Stop this nonsense about Ploughmen. It turns me right up. I wonder what happened to bread and cheese? *Local* cheese I mean – yes, there is one for *your* region. Hands up those who serve it.

8 The Police

As we shall see, the selling of liquor and the attitudes of Authority are intricately entwined. It is a jungle, a minefield. You are going to have to learn to tread warily, to balance more surely than any tightrope walker, in order to avoid not just a few pitfalls, but disasters and catastrophes. And this is particularly true in your dealings with the police.

Policeman and Publican – An Uneasy Relationship

It is, alas, very rare indeed for any licensee not to fall foul of the police in some way throughout his career in the trade, especially nowadays. Now I do not mean that you will break the law intentionally, or even turn a blind eye to some of its lunacies; what I do mean is that it is virtually impossible to maintain what used to be called 'a clean sheet' if your local police are determined to be difficult, if not downright threatening.

Now I am sorry to have to say this but gone are the days when there was an easy relationship of tolerance (even, on occasion, a 'bending' of the law) between police and publican; a sort of *quid pro quo* which recognized that both sides could be of value to each other because of their local knowledge and, above all, because of the licensee's position as a good listener and a close observer of his customers, regular or casual. Quite what has soured this relationship is difficult to say. Certainly not the landlord. It may be the drink-driving laws and the fact that the moral standards and attitudes of police recruits – and many of their senior officers – are not quite as exemplary as they used to be. However, a chasm now exists between the two sides where a small ditch used to be the case, and then only on the rare occasion.

It is important to understand that the licensee is a convenient whipping-boy. When I was a lad a man who could not 'hold his drink' was almost a social outcast, hardly a man at all. Nowadays, that man is 'ill' – the victim of the seller, and even the manufacturer, of drink. Publicans may soon face prosecution for initially selling alcohol (albeit unwittingly) to anyone who is later found to be 'one over the eight' or to a motor-vehicle driver found to be over the limit. It is bad enough for a licensee to be expected to possess powers of divination as to whether youngsters are under or over eighteen; he will soon be expected mentally to breath-test all his customers before pulling them a pint. It is a sad development as it makes a publican's job increasingly difficult while allowing the police the scapegoat they nowadays so badly need.

The Magistrates Court

Your first meeting with the police will probably be via your local magistrates court when you apply for your protection order. This order allows you legally to sell drink when you take over your pub for the first time. It will require your presence in court, as well as that of the outgoing landlord, who will state formally that he agrees to your taking over the licence. You will also have to testify that you will run a proper pub; the magistrates will probably then give you a short lecture about under-age drinking and, often, the widespread evils of alcohol in general. This is a formality. The real evidence as to whether you are a 'fit and proper person' to hold a liquor licence at all will be given by the local police inspector, or someone under him, who will say they have made enquiries about you and that there is no trace of a criminal record or any other reason why you should not have the licence. This statement will have been the result of your solicitor's filling in the correct forms of application for a protection order the moment it became fairly certain that you were going to be the new landlord. The procedure is the same whether you are buying a free house or becoming a brewery tenant, though in the latter case the brewery's legal department will attend to such matters.

Once again I must stress the need for a good solicitor – someone who knows the locality and knows all the problems you may have to face.

This first appearance in court will be by no means your last – though I do hope all of them will remain a mere formality. the protection order will run until the next full sitting of the licensing magistrates (or what used to be called Brewster Sessions) when your annual licence will be confirmed. It is the usual custom, even if you are not a member of the Licensed Victuallers Association, to have all these formal renewals handled by just one solicitor who will act for all the licensees in the district. This mass application also covers the statutory 'extensions of hours' which will apply locally throughout the trade for bank holidays, Christmas, New Year and so on. It will not cover special occasions which you, as a landlord, may wish to have for various private functions or special events. The cost is minimal, under £10 a year including the legal fees. Once again your own solicitor will know the form and will advise you. If he professes ignorance of any customary practice, then you have the wrong solicitor, or he is not local enough.

It is important for you to remember that whatever you do to your pub, even if you want to change or alter a bit of the bar or even the toilets, permission will have to be sought from the court (not to mention the other authorities such as Planning, Environmental Health and so on) and properly drawn plans for such alterations will have to be submitted. It is a wearisome business, but unavoidable. I should also stress that all gaming machines (such as one-armed bandits, pool tables and so on) are also subject to the proper licences from the court. In other words, *do nothing* without asking your solicitor or the local police first. In that way you will avoid the risk of running foul of the law unwittingly.

The Boys in Blue Call By …
Soon after you move into your pub the police will call to see you, and to see your licence. They are checking officially to see if it really is you, the man who appeared in court, who holds the licence. But unofficially it is a

nosey-parker look-see to find out the sort of man (or woman) you are and how you are likely to run the place. Remember: it is an offence to offer a police officer a drink when he is on duty. And however enthusiastic and new you are to the trade, and however much you wish to make the police welcome, make sure that if you have young children they are not behind the bar at any time other than for the 'purposes of moving from one part of the building to another'. Even your own flesh and blood are deemed to be in need of protection from the evils of drink, drinking and drinkers, and your visitors may well not take kindly to being introduced to the family – an introduction that in other circumstances may well be considered good manners.

It is quite possible that the officers will be pleasant and courteous. It is sad to have to make such a statement. At one time you could have guaranteed it; courtesy to the public reaped rich rewards in terms of public appreciation and help. This is not any longer deemed necessary by most constabularies. As an aside I once had just such a visit, by an inspector and a sergeant, just two days after I had moved in as a licensee. I thought they were pleasant and helpful and I made the mistake of thinking that I had started off on the right foot. The following day I received notification that I was committing an offence by not displaying my name as licensee on the statutory notice above the main door. Many years ago the police, unless they were uncharacteristically bone-headed, would have pointed it out with a laugh when they left and not wasted their time or mine by a 'warning of possible prosecution', especially in the case of a new landlord who had only just moved in.

Drink-Driving

On the very serious matter of drink-drinking offences (though keep the problem in perspective by bearing in mind that fewer than ten per cent of all traffic accidents in the UK involve any form of alcohol and that in many of those accidents the only person involved is the drinker) it is customary now for the better pubs to display a polite notice near the main door offering to call a taxi for any customer who requires it. On special occasions, like

Christmas or the New Year, some publicans lay on a 'courtesy bus' to take all their local customers home at closing time. Both examples illustrate the effect the drink-driving laws are having on our pubs and it is a foolish landlord who ignores them. I am not suggesting you should go too far 'over the top' by quizzing everyone at your bar as to whether they have a car parked outside and inviting them not to take any more alcohol, although I am advising you to stock non-alcoholic drinks which are prominently displayed and fairly priced. You may feel that the offer to call at taxi, along with a polite note to the effect that you feel you have a responsibility to your customers as well as to the public at large – as is displayed at one pub I know at Fletching in Sussex – is sufficient, or you may wish to go much further as one man I know who keeps a very close eye on all customers and demands their car keys if he feels they are over the limit, threatening to call the police if the customer refuses. It is an unpleasant situation and one which only you can resolve. One thing, as I said before, is certain. If you even unknowingly and innocently supply drink to a driver who is found to be over the limit the police will make a much greater misery of your life than they will, very often, of the motorist.

Under-age Drinking

Under-age drinking is almost as much a problem as over-the-limit drinking. It is an offence for anyone to buy alcohol if they are under the age of eighteen. It is also an offence to sell it to them. Licensees in some areas are so worried about this that the Licensed Victuallers Association encourages some form of identity-card scheme to be issued to young people who are, in fact, over eighteen but look younger. Whether you agree with this is your affair although it seems pretty ludicrous to me. Why not have a national identity-card system for all citizens, as many foreign countries do, and be done with it?

This problem is yet another worry for the licensee, especially if you run a pub tucked away in a town or in country not far from a town where there is a large population of senior schoolboys and girls – as there are in many areas possessed of public schools. It is almost impossible to tell whether anyone is definitely under age and even the politest enquiry often leads to an outraged reply, whether innocent or not. One thing is certain: if anyone under age is caught by the police on their way home, say, who confesses to having been drinking in your pub it is likely that the police will summons you straight away. There is no easy solution for you as a landlord – whatever police, magistrates or do-gooders may say. In my own experience I have seen schoolboys, wearing blazers and carrying caps, paraded in court in an effort to trap a landlord on a charge of selling alcohol to 'obvious' under-age drinkers, a trick intended to bamboozle the magistrates. Mercifully, the trick does not always work, as many, if not most, magistrates are too wise and reasonable to be taken in.

If in doubt, never serve a youngster any alcohol unless he can prove he is eighteen or over, and make sure someone who may well be of a correct age is not buying drinks for his under-age mates – a very common trick and practised even by some parents, who should know better.

I cannot stress the problems the law on youngsters can cause landlords and the old adage: if in doubt, chuck it out applies equally well to children as it does to foodstuffs or drink which is not a fresh as it should be. Most landlords get round this question simply by banning all youngsters from their bars, even if they are legally allowed to be there once they are fourteen, or at the age of sixteen 'may be sold beer, porter, cider or perry for consumption at a meal in a part of the premises usually set apart for the service of meals and which is not a bar'. You will have to make up your own mind. You will have to be discreet and not dictatorial but you have the upper hand for legally you have the ultimate say in which members of the public shall or shall not be on your property. Remember that it is not just a question of a fine (anything from £100 to £400), but your whole future livelihood. You can lose your licence if you break the law a second time.

'After-Hours' Drinking

The third common problem which might involve you unpleasantly with the police is the hoary old one of late-night, or 'after-hours' drinking.

Once again times have changed, as they say. Drinking after closing time, especially in the evening, has been a hallowed tradition of British life ever since the crazy pattern of licensing laws was promulgated during the First World War. Indeed, it was the direct result of such restrictions on the right of a man to sell and a man to buy a drink whenever they so wished. Admittedly, with the new 'permitted hours' between 11 a.m. and 11 p.m. the problem has decreased during the day but in the countryside especially (there are too many 'snoopers' about in towns) it is still pretty prevalent in certain establishments.

To this tradition, although strictly speaking against the law, the police for the most part turned a blind eye, but on certain conditions. In the first place late drinking had to be conducted wisely, prudently and without disturbance to members of the general public; secondly, there had to be a tacit understanding and trust between police and publican, allowing the former to curtail the extent or the frequency; thirdly, it was conducted without prejudice to the police and their authority and only among close-knit local villagers, groups of customers or people unlikely to 'blab' or give the game away – that is, tactful, adult men and women.

The advantages were manifold. Because late drinking would go on, whatever the law said and however vigilant the police force, it was convenient to have it confined to one particular pub in any one area. This pub was always known to the local bobby. Indeed, the custom was not without its attractions to that stalwart himself, who might well find himself inexplicably possessed of a raging thirst an hour or so before his duty shift ended at midnight or 1 a.m. in the morning. But because of his privileged position, the landlord of that pub could be warned in advance of any 'head office' blitz in that area, in which senior officers from headquarters, reinforced with young and eager constables, could move in once a year and blanket search every hostelry within a fifteen-mile radius. In such circumstances the local pubs (because no malefactors were discovered) earned good marks in the annual police superintendent's report to the licensing justices, the local bobby earned good marks for his vigilance and skill in keeping control of his local hostelries and good, honest publicans and drinkers could sleep easily and deeply on their one early night of the year.

But picture what happened when landlords changed or bobbies were posted elsewhere and their places taken by a new one? Late drinking would resume, as night follows day. But where? That was the trouble. It could take many wasted man hours to track down the culprit, to find out whether this or that pub was the regular place, to find out whether it was just the odd occasion that one particular bar was filled with loud cheerfulness at ten past midnight. Far better to have it all confined to just one trustworthy pub and publican; to know that a small word in an ear would ensure rigid enforcement of the law for at least one night by the licensee, for reasons appreciated by all concerned.

In this way a fine balance was kept between police and publican. It is a balance, I do assure you with great sadness, that rarely exists nowadays. It is my duty to warn you of the risks of permitting after-hours drinking – it could lead to the loss of your licence and livelihood, and it is a risk I would counsel you against taking, if only for the fact that the police in various areas are now not above 'rigging' late drinking by deliberately turning a blind eye initially, so that later they can obtain a conviction against some luckless publican in order to enhance their 'crime' figures or further their personal careers. And do not think you can get round the law by claiming all the people in your bar at midnight are just friends having a party at your expense. No copper is that stupid – especially when he has heard the till merrily ringing away and his local knowledge tells him you have never set eyes on the bunch before in your whole life.

Now I have been purposefuly 'anti' police to rub home the point that you can no longer afford to trust them, as once any decent citizen could. But that does not mean that all of them are like that. You may well be lucky enough to live in an area where happy co-operation exists between the police and the publican (as well as the public). I am not suggesting all licensees break the law and all coppers indulge them. Not at all. But peaceful co-existence, understanding and trust is the order of the day. I suspect that such areas are diminishing in number and size, but if you do take a pub in such an area, I would ask you earnestly not to abuse your position, or take liberties with the law.

Regional Quirks
It would be impossible in a book of this size and scope to cover the entire field of licensing law, but the points I have mentioned are certainly the most important. I do stress that your own local solicitor is the person to guide you through the minefield. There are, however, wide-ranging interpretations and local traditions in the observance of such laws. In some areas there may be all sorts of pointless restrictions on 'extensions' – permission granted by magistrates for special occasions, when drinking can be allowed after normal closing time for some important holiday, local festival or private 'do', such as a wedding. Both the local police and the justices make full use of their own powers and opinions in such cases, and whereas in one area extensions are easy to come by, they may be almost impossible in an adjoining territory. Towns separated by only five miles of countryside, or boroughs by a line down the middle of a street can be quite different. As a stranger you will need your solicitor's help continually in your early days, though if you are a brewery tenant life will be made that much easier since much of the legal work and advice will be clear-cut. As the owner of a free house you are very much on your own; as the tenant of a brewery you will have to observe strict rules laid down about your behaviour and legal obligations and if you do fall foul of the law for any serious offence (such as late drinking) you may find your tenancy in jeopardy. I suppose the old adage is the best one to follow: if in doubt, find out.

As an example certain areas of Britain may differ in regard to 'permitted games'. Not only is credit disallowed on licensed premises, gambling for money is also prohibited, yet in parts of Britain it is quite normal to see curious card games, or dominoes, being played loudly and at great speed with no attempt at hiding small piles of money on the tables. These practices are often of strictly local tradition, just as skittle alleys are in the West Country, or outdoor bowling greens around Carlisle. After years of running a pub in the West Country I still never managed to fathom the card game played in my bar by some of the locals, yet I have to confess I would no more have dreamed of banning it than the police or magistrates.

Unless you have a large pub in the centre of a city it is unlikely you will be bothered by prostitution, but knowingly permitting prostitutes to use your premises could lose you your licence. Drugs can also be a problem. Be vigilant and under no circumstances whatsoever tolerate any form of drug peddling or drug taking. If you have good reason to suspect any one person or group of people I honestly believe it to be your duty to inform the police immediately. Also be careful in letting any room you may have for 'private' parties – most of them are perfectly all right but there is a tendency now for video equipment to be set up for the showing of blue movies. This may not be strictly illegal, but it can get a publican a bad name very quickly so you want to make quite sure that the establishment you are running never ever gets near to becoming what used to be called a house of ill-repute.

The Management Has the Right ...
As a licensee you can refuse to serve anyone to whom you object. You do not even have to specify a reason. This is a right you will find useful when faced with drunkenness or aggression. Sadly the two often walk hand in hand. It is unlikely that you will escape these sort of problems during your career, however tactful and careful you are.

Those two words are, however, a good safeguard. Always remain calm. Never raise your voice. Never threaten violence, whatever the threat has been to you. If you cannot contain the problem, tell the miscreant, or even a number of them, quietly and firmly that you will call the police if they do not leave not only your premises but the area outside. If they persist tell a member of staff, or even someone you know well who is in the bar, to go to the telephone and dial 999. It is unfortunate if you are alone or have no one to ask as it is important that you do not leave the bar – your absence will tend to exacerbate the situation and may even lead to damage. Remember, the police have a duty to protect you and other members of the public and they will not later look askance at your request for assistance providing they know that you are a responsible, decent licensee. Indeed, their attendance may well insure your being left alone by nuisance-makers in the future.

But do not be misled into thinking that men are the worst culprits. Sadly, women can be a whole lot more of a problem. I have had women break up the ladies' toilets, even smashing pot plants, mirrors and light-fittings. It is a particularly unpleasant problem for you as a male licensee and for your male staff. Never ever touch a drunken woman. Always get help, even from a female customer, if only to avoid any accusation of indelicate behaviour. In the case of one woman who clung to an armchair in my bar, hysterically refusing to leave, my wife 'refereed' while two (male) customers and myself picked the chair up, complete with woman, and deposited her outside in the lane. Mercifully the weather was extremely cold and she came to her senses quite quickly. But do not expect always to get off lightly. However tactful and kind you are things can still go wrong very easily and on one occasion I was punched in the face by a drunken man whom I thought to be one of the most mild-mannered men imaginable. I was congratulated sincerely by other customers on the way I had tactfully handled that particular situation. I hoped it made the black eye less conspicuous but the possession of a 'shiner' may well have served as a warning to anyone else for some days afterwards.

Neither of those incidents, nor any others, necessitated our calling the police but you may well not be so fortunate. Your own tact and experience will lead you to realize quickly how serious, or potentially serious, any situation may be. In many cases a quiet word will suffice, or even a firm warning that such behaviour will not be tolerated. But if in doubt, get assistance. It is too late once the place (and you) have been torn apart.

If and when these incidents do happen they are of acute embarrassment to other customers, however well the situation has been handled. So what do you do? What did we do after the woman had been carried out, after I had got a black eye?

There is only one thing you can do, inadequate though it will be. You go round to all the other customers and you apologize personally. You do not try to escape blame or to apportion it. You do not run down the man or woman or group who have behaved badly. You simply apologize for the embarrassment and upset your customers have suffered. You certainly do not offer them a free drink (unless the circumstances were exceptional and all their glasses had been smashed). And you hope that time alone will prove to them that you were right and innocent and the disturbance was not of your making. But please do not make a great issue out of it – either to yourself, by cursing yourself for not seeing it coming, or for not handling the situation correctly. And never refer to it in public again. People will soon forget any unpleasantness and, providing you have behaved along the lines I suggested, will come to regard you – 'their' landlord – with considerable respect and, quite possibly, affection.

A Positive Note

Of course, the police can, on occasions, be of valuable assistance to you, and the cultivation of good relations with them is at least well worth a try. In most areas it will prove not only a sound investment but will lead to enjoyable friendships, as well as occasionally being a profitable one, for the constabulary are still, by and large, a convivial bunch, and they may well hold the odd party or celebration at your pub. Try by all reasonable means to get them on your side, to show them you are a responsible and understanding landlord. It will make life easier (and much more pleasant) all round.

9   The Implications of Your Licence

The previous chapter dealing with the police is merely an introduction to the bureaucracy you will face once you open the doors of a pub. And not only do you have to have a notice outside those doors saying who you are and what you are licensed to sell (such as beers, wines and spirits) but you must also have a notice just inside those doors which proclaims the names of the owners of the business which have been registered under the Business Names Act – you can normally get the appropriate form from your bank. But in this chapter let us take a look at the myriad officials you are going to deal with, and provide records for, ranging from the EHO to the Inland Revenue.

Visits from Council Officials
We have already met the Environmental Health Officer, but let me jog your memory by repeating that he has an interest not only in the food side of your business (if any) but also in the bar, drinks storage areas and general cleanliness and suitability of any part of the property used by the public, including the toilets. He will also want to investigate where and how you keep your refuse and even the condition of outbuildings, in case they are havens of rest for vermin. You may also need to meet the local planning officer if you are proposing to make any alterations, which will in turn entail contact with the building control inspector who will want to ensure his fourpennorth is put in when it comes to construction work, drainage and so on. But just bear in mind that the licensing magistrates and the police will also want a say in any alterations proposed. Incidentally, a pub sign on your actual building (unless it is ludicrous in claim and size) is

not controlled by local planning regulations, but you will need permission if you want to advertise your pub in any way (say at the end of a lane to it) or for a sign which is free-standing away from the property.

The local trading standards officer may well make a call on you to ensure you are displaying a price list in the bar and that if you serve food there is a menu, also with prices, outside the door where the public can inspect it. And some time after you move in two unsmiling officials from HM Customs and Excise measures department will call to test the optics or spirit measures you use. They will be carrying a most marvellous mahogany box which opens to reveal a velvet-lined, compartmentalized set of clear-glass measuring phials. They will then solemnly pour into these phials the liquor from your own optics, and will then pour the liquor from the phials back into your bottles. You have nothing to fear from this process unless you have illegally broken the sealed optics to insert pebbles into the containers – a trick which originally caused that whole Customs department to be formed. Their visit will take about two minutes. They will show you their warrant cards and they will endure silently and without emotion the usual badinage from your customers about what they do with the 'heel taps' left in their phials at the end of the day. If you do not have a prominently displayed statutory notice declaring the size of the spirit measures served in your bar they will point this out to you and 'advise' you to get one straight away. They will leave as quickly as they arrived and you will not expect to see them for another two years. But never, ever be tempted to give short measures or touch optics. You will assuredly lose your licence when they catch you. And quite right too.

Licensing Laws

Licensing law in Scotland (as any reasonable, cultured person would expect) is a lot more reasonable, logical and sensible than it is in England. Wales has its own attitudes and in 1989 voted by a national referendum to open pubs on Sundays. I think this must demonstrate more than anything else the stupid, not to say ludicrous, manner in which licensing law is governed in Britain, making us the laughing-stock to the rest of Europe. Can you imagine, for instance, not being able to have a drink in neighbouring Antibes? Or Benidorm being 'dry' and Alicante 'open all hours'. As a licensee you are going to have to get used to the illogical, the insane. You are going to have to get used to a local police inspector, whose total knowledge of the world may well have been confined within a small area of prejudice, religious bigotry and poor education, actually having the right to stand up before some magistrates and object to your perfectly reasonable, logical and proper application for, say, an extension of a drinks licence for some national, or even traditional but very local event, and telling them why they should not grant it. And on the whole, they will agree. It is an appalling negation of freedom in every way and yet you are going to have to learn to live with it. We shall look at the ludicrous situation in greater detail later but until England and Wales achieve the perfectly ordinary, logical and sensible attitudes that prevail in Scotland the actual seller of alcohol will be subjected to hypocritical regulation without any base in logic, reason or statistical research. To the authorities, do-gooders and hop-heads the way to prevent alcohol abuse is to ban alcohol – an idea which spectacularly failed to work in one historic instance, as we all know.

VAT

But talk of HM Customs and Excise necessarily leads on to the VAT people. They are going to be a burden you must carry for the rest of your business life, if only because their requirements, demands, rules and regulations are unstintingly applied whatever your circumstances. If, say, your returns are late because you have had a serious heart-attack or are in intensive care following a traffic accident, you will still be threatened and certainly fined. Even death itself is no reasonable excuse to the VAT people. So who are these people and what makes them such monsters?

Value Added Tax is a tax on your turnover. It is a tax which you are expected to exact from your customers and pay over to the Customs and Excise every three months. You are essentially an unpaid tax collector. In 1990 the threshold at which VAT of fifteen per cent became payable was set at £25,400 per annum. You may expect it to keep pace roughly with inflation each year.

In theory the system is simple. For every £1 you take into your till, whether it is for food, drink or any other service, you give 15p to the Government. If you have paid any VAT in order to provide those goods and services to the public, you can set that off against the 15p. Thus if you sell a drink for £1, and therefore owe 15p in VAT, but the drink has cost you 50p to buy, including VAT of 6.25p, you can deduct that 6.25p from the 15p, paying just the balance to Customs and Excise. Nothing could be easier, could it? What do you mean, there is no such thing as 6.25p? Nonsense. HM Customs and Excise do not recognize the buttons on any calculator – all VAT transactions are calculated at 3/23rds – thus the VAT on £1 (or 100p) is actually 13.04p and not 15p as I said above. For accounting purposes the VAT inspectors expect you to round down or up. Still think it easy?

However, VAT will be a nightmare. It will require the keeping of every single monetary transaction for six years and the minute recording of these transactions every three months on to a form of enormous complexity. The language is arcane and confusing, as every good civil servant's inventions should be. Thus what you sell to the public is called 'outputs'. What you buy yourself from, say, a brewery, is called 'inputs'. The value of the outputs minus the value of the inputs is the amount of tax you must pay every quarter. It never occurred to the VAT authorities to think up simpler, more obvious and understandable words. Customs and Excise are probably the last Government department to refuse to adopt Plain English as standard. But complaining about their obfuscation and your lack of understanding will do you no good at all. You will be penalized by a surcharge of up to thirty per cent of the VAT owed if returns are late. You must keep exact records of both outputs and inputs and they have to be written into a VAT book for regular examination by VAT inspectors. You are obliged to register by law. You will be given a VAT number which must be quoted on everything. If you knowingly defraud the VAT inspectors the fines are punitive and you may go to prison. The harsh penalties and rigid regulations are, HM Customs and Excise say, because VAT is first taken from a customer whether that customer likes it or not and if it is not paid over in good faith to Customs and Excise you are not defrauding the authorities so much as committing a fraud on the public by taking fifteen per cent of their money for your own purposes. Be that as it may you will curse the day it was ever thought of and the extra work it will involve.

A word of warning. Make up your VAT records at least every week. If you leave them until your return becomes due, you are going to get into a terrible mess. Buy a proper VAT book from a good stationer's and use it for every monetary transaction, whether it incurs VAT or not. The Simplex series is excellent and there is even a special licensee's account book with columns directly revelant to your own operation. If you keep a book like this meticulously it will make your book-keeping much easier. The VAT inspectors will not mind that the book contains information irrelevant to them. Indeed, it is a token of your good faith that you are prepared to show all your business transactions without fear. It also establishes the extent of your business.

You will find the VAT inspectors for the most part charming and affable. They go in pairs, it is said, for the same reason secret police go in pairs – none can be trusted on their own and the extra fingers and toes of a second person is necessary for their arithmetic. The inspectors will call to see you and check your books around the third quarter after you started in business. They will telephone you first and ask if such and such a time is convenient. They will require a room of their own, and all your records. They will spend some hours at their task. They will not accept anything like a free drink or food but they appreciate the offer of coffee or tea at the appropriate time. When they have finished their work they will invite you to clarify any questions they may have. They will advise you if you have made mistakes and they will do their level best to help you avoid making any in the future. They may even praise you for your book-keeping, in which case people like me will wonder why you are working in a pub when you should be working in an accountant's office, a job which is better paid and has shorter hours.

At the end of their inspection and appraisal they will inform you whether you owe them money and how much. But they may well tell you you have paid too much VAT and merit a reimbursement. Either way they will be right. You are talking to experts – and you would do well to remember that they are experts in your trade. They will have inspected dozens and dozens of pubs, clubs, restaurants and the like and they will have developed a 'nose' for the honest business (even though some mistakes can be found) and an awareness for what is not right or does not ring true.

I have to say honestly that on one occasion I was found to have paid too much tax – they discovered they owed me more than £700, which was a pleasant surprise – and on another occasion that I had paid £1,200 too little. The latter was an unpleasant shock. Both inspectors said how sorry they were to have found such a large error and both said it had nothing to do with dishonesty, just stupidity. They laughed heartily at their joke, finished their tea and biscuits, and two days later a demand for immediate payment of £1,200 back tax arrived. On the final day of the grace given to me for payment the hard men arrived to collect a cheque. The collectors are totally different to the inspectors. They are unpleasant, aggressive and humour- less. If you fail to pay they have a bailiff with a distress warrant already waiting in their car. The bailiff is a permanent fixture in the back. They were not at all pleased when I asked them if they ever took him out and dusted him down. They took their cheque, wrote a receipt, told me that if the cheque bounced the bailiff would be let loose and I would have to pay statutory penalties in addition to the arrears. They left without even saying goodbye.

The number of businesspeople in Britain who can recount similar horror stories probably runs into thousands every year. Yet VAT is not really a matter for your accountant, although he will probably do it for you if you insist and can afford his fees. VAT is a chore, an extra hassle, and I would strongly advise you to find a part-time book-keeper, perhaps even a retired bank manager, who will come in once a month and do all your account books for you. He or she will be worth every penny you pay them. I personally would prefer to pay a book-keeper than a cellarman or barman. But that is maybe because I am innumerate and uninterested in figures, whereas I find the other two jobs absorbing.

The Inland Revenue

The Inland Revenue, quite obviously, will be interested in your business affairs, and good book-keeping will not only help them but also lessen your accountant's fees, since he should have less trouble making up your accounts.

Do try to maintain good relations with your local Inland Revenue office and start off by telling them, either by letter or in person, who you are, where you are and what you are going to do. They will also want to know which office handled your previous tax affairs. Remember the simple rules: if you are successful then you are going to have to pay some form of what is broadly called income tax. You cannot escape it. But it may be some years before you have to pay a penny in actuality – your myriad business expenses will all be taken into account. On the other hand, good relations with your local Inland Revenue office will never come amiss. And make sure your accountant enjoys a good reputation with that office as well. It saves everyone trouble all round. Once again, I hope your accountant is as local as your solicitor, and has good knowledge of the area.

Gaming Machines

It may be useful to jog your memory about gaming machines and similar amusements such as pool tables. You will need, as I said, permission from the licensing justices before you can install them, which will involve the police. Do not be tempted to put such machines in and *then* ask permission. You cannot afford to upset authority. Prizes are laid down by law and the people who lease out the machines will explain the complex mix of money pay-outs and tokens which you are allowed. In reality you as landlord merely take a 'cut' of what the machines take, the rest going to the company which owns them. Legal permission is not needed for vending machines, however, such as those for cigarettes, condoms in either gents' or ladies' toilets (becoming increasingly the norm) or toiletries, but make sure such machines do not cause any obstruction of public walkways, otherwise fire safety regulations may be involved.

Music
Finally a word about music in your pub, or, indeed, any form of entertainment. Live musical performances do not require a licence or permission providing no more than two people perform at any one time. If you have a band, or a group of entertainers, you will need permission from the magistrates, which will also involve seeking the views of the police, as well as the fire safety officer. You will then be into the realms of audience limitation, proper emergency exits, lighting and a host of other problems. Not for you, I would suggest, starting out in your new business. Leave that to the big chain pubs or until you are firmly established.

But in the absence of live music you may want 'piped' music. This is not free, however. It may not need a magistrates' licence but it will need a licence from the Performing Rights Society (PRS) This organization keeps a very close eye on new landlords, going through the court lists and visiting pubs at least once a year, to ensure that if you do have piped music you are paying a percentage for the privilege. Do not try to get out of this. If you continue to flout them the local representative of the PRS will simply take out a summons against you – an expensive and unnecessary business when it can so easily be avoided.

Now I have only touched on officialdom here. As a licensee you will be expected to be an absolute expert on everything which may affect you. VAT and the Inland Revenue, the Weights and Measures Act, the Health and Safety at Work Act, a number of employment acts, the

Misuse of Drugs Act, Environmental Health regulations, fire precautions, building control regulations, the Race Relations Act, the Wages Inspectorate and a host of other rules, measures, regulations, dos and don'ts, including, of course, the various licensing acts. None of the officials administering all this bureaucracy is concerned with anyone else's job: each of them is a specialist. Lucky old you. You are meant to know the whole lot!

10 Staff

Let us now consider the whole question of staff in your new pub – possibly one of the biggest expenses and headaches of your business life. From the point of view of paperwork you must keep a wages book if you employ full-time staff and you must also deduct PAYE, National Insurance and so on. The local office of the Inland Revenue will provide all the information you want, along with tables showing what has to be deducted. Do not hesitate to seek advice from the Inland Revenue, for they would prefer you to ask now rather than get into a muddle later. You also owe it to your staff to ensure they get their wages correctly and properly paid, without having to worry about paying too much or too little tax and so on.

But in all matters concerning staff I would urge you to go to your local Jobcentre, which stock the special booklets issued by the Department of Employment. These are well written, clear and useful. They cover every aspect of staff – employer relations imaginable, from recruiting people to sacking them and every legal aspect in-between.

'Sitting' Employees

We will start with a warning. Suppose the pub you are taking over already has full-time staff. Perhaps the licensee employed a full-time manager or barman or even cook or waitress. If yours is such a place you will probably feel better and easier to begin with a clean sheet, so to speak, and let go the previous incumbents. You might well be right, but, alas, the law does not allow it. If you take over an existing business which employs full-time staff you take them over too; and if such staff have been there a number of years it will cost you an arm and a leg in redundancy payments to get rid of them. You should have thought of that aspect long before you contemplated taking any pub.

But it is quite probable that if this is your first venture you will not want or need to employ full-time staff at all.

Casual Staff

The entire catering and drinks trade in Britain would collapse without 'casual' staff. By its very nature the trade demands, and can absorb, thousands of women who either want or have to work odd hours because of children, yet who need the money (however little) or interest a part-time job gives them. Many men also need the extra money to be gained by working in bars or restaurants in the evening or at weekends. The term used, somewhat unfairly I always think, is 'moonlighting'. This word applied originally to those people who worked for themselves 'out of hours' in the trade of their main full-time employer and were thus in competition with him. I think most people who work in pubs nowadays do so out of absolute necessity – a means of paying the rent, as they say.

As a result, casual staff are often very vulnerable. Employers cash in on this vulnerability in a way that I find distasteful and distressing, changing their working hours without thought, 'forgetting' to pay them, paying them late or paying them 'by mistake' a lower rate than agreed (all tricks that are much more common than supposed) and generally treating them like lackeys. Because of the fragile relationship which exists between 'casual' staff and any employer, many employers seek to exploit the embarrassment people naturally feel if they complain about 'mistakes' in their pay, hours or so on. Even so, it is those same employers who complain most bitterly about lack of 'staff loyalty' or how casuals constantly leave and have to be replaced. Can you wonder at it?

The Sixteen-Hour Rule

But let us start with the law, even though it is generally ignored. If you employ somebody for sixteen hours a week or less such people are in general outside the scope of the

Inland Revenue, the National Insurance rules or any regulations which govern full-time employment, pensions, holidays entitlements and so on. These workers are, in the eyes of the law, 'non people' and as such have absolutely no protection against exploitation by the employer. In general these people work about ten hours a week for not much more than £2 an hour, which is in fact way below the statutory rate for labour in any industry. And to add insult to injury the fact that such people have to work regularly for you for five years before they are even entitled to a written contract and job description just illustrates how low down the scale of importance and care our industry's major workforce comes in public and parliamentary esteem.

Even so, I firmly believe that there is no reason for casual staff to be treated to appallingly. So I am simply going to suggest how *you* might care to treat them and, should you follow my advice, see whether it pays off for you, as it always did (mercifully) for us.

Say What the Job Entails

In the first place never mislead any applicant as to the job on offer and how you expect it to be done. We should all avoid the modern euphemisms by which a practical hygiene operative means drain cleaner and an experienced executive manager to 'head up a close-knit team of practical hygiene operatives' means a foreman. So if you want a cleaner, make sure you say it is a cleaner you want. Sounds simple but, alas, it very rarely happens. The worst mistake you can make, of course, is to limit the job description too much, especially when you are new to the business. Now you may indeed want just a cleaner, but to do only the public areas? Not your own quarters now and again? Never touch the kitchen? Or sweep down the yard, or scrub out the larder? Do you see how complicated it can suddenly become? Surely it would be better to explain all the multifarious duties in the first place. You may, for instance, never intend asking your cleaner to 'pop upstairs' to make someone's bed, or just dust your living-room, but you may not have thought that one day you and your spouse will be run ragged trying to cope with a surprise visit from the Environmental Health Officer on market day, the busiest in the week. But if you, did explain to her, in the first place, that the main job was to keep the bar areas, toilets and passageways spick and span, but now and again you would not mind some help in the kitchen or even in your own quarters when she had time it would avoid all sorts of resentments later on. Do not leave matters to chance. After all, if the person in question said he or she would do the bar, toilets and passageways, but under no circumstances anything or anywhere else, then at least both of you would know where you stood. It is the loading of other, unexpected work on to someone's shoulders at the last minute which people dislike, as it is, in effect, a 'try on' which people may feel they have to accept just because they would be embarrassed to say no.

So the sort of person you will want to employ, I would suggest, would come under the heading of 'general help'. Why not call it that? And make absolutely certain that both you and the applicant know what the term covers. Discuss and agree not just the 'rate for the job' and whether they are to be on probation for a month or so, but the exact terms and conditions. Show them the problems, the areas of work. Do not limit either your thinking or theirs. Suppose you really want someone to help out in the bar and wait at table. If you limit your thinking to that you may well miss out on the fact that the man or woman standing beside you is a talented cook, or once worked as a book-keeper in a bank. Just think what a godsend that could be.

Above all, aim to *involve* your staff in the whole business of running your pub. Make them feel an essential part of the whole operation. Do not give them the idea that they may be no good at something else, or should not be interested in some other aspect or should keep their noses out of things which do not concern them. You are too small an outfit to assume such attitudes. You are going to need all the help you can get, from every direction. As a personal example we once had a marvellous gardener. He would appear in the kitchen every morning and ask what vegetables we wanted and reappear sometime later with the order. But he had an uncanny knack of sensing when the pressure was on and regularly would return to the kitchen later on to help with the dishing-up on to plates, the washing-up or even with the preparation of extra potatoes and so forth. He was worth his weight in gold. But supposing we had regarded him as 'just the gardener'. What a mass of talent and ability we would have thrown away or never discovered. The important point about this story, however, should not be lost: our gardener *enjoyed* being part of the whole outfit. He revelled in it. He also earned good money and he had a share of the *tronc*, a system we adopted by which money left in tips was distributed among the staff.

Appearance and Behaviour

A very common mistake newcomers (and even old hands) make when employing people is to forget, either deliberately or by mistake, to say how they should dress. If, for instance, you run a spit and sawdust boozer where everyone dresses in scruffy, mucky clothes, then your bar staff might look out of place in anything else, though I, for one, would doubt it. Yet how many times have you walked into quite a smart bar to find the woman behind in faded jeans and her hair full of hedgerow? Very often, I am afraid. So you must make up your mind not only as to the sort of place you are running, but how you want it to appear to the customer. It is no good a member of your bar staff coming to work on a Monday dressed in torn jeans and then on Friday saying he or she looks awful and should change. You had no business to allow them to think that scruffiness would be in order at any time. Your duty is to tell your employees from the start just how you expect them to look when on duty. Mind you, if someone turns up for an interview looking scruffy I would get rid of them on the spot. Do not even consider people who look slovenly, act with ill-grace, are sullen or resentful. Remember, your staff are your ambassadors. If they are disagreeable to you then so will they be to your livelihood – your customers. Do not jeopardize it by taking on the first person who walks in through the door, just in case you do not get any more. There will always be someone else, and even if there is not, that is still no excuse for employing someone who is a threat to your whole existence.

As an example I knew a place sometime back where the food was really quite good. One day a dreadful harridan of a woman appeared in the dining area. She turned out to be the cook. Her appearance and attitude (she had come to have a public row with the landlord because the washer-up had failed to materialize) certainly put me off eating there ever again, or even calling in for a pint. Now it so happened that the landlord fired her there and then, on the spot. He refused to countenance her appearing in public looking like she did. She had no business to appear in the bar area, he told her. She let everyone know in no uncertain terms that nobody was going to dictate to her what she wore in her own kitchen. The landlord pointed out that it was not her kitchen, it was in fact his and told her to get out. I think she was glad to go and the landlord to see the back of her. But who was to blame for such a charmless scene? Well, I have to tell you – the landlord, in my opinion. He had no business to employ her in the first place without specifying what she should wear, how she should look when on duty in his pub. I have no idea whether she turned up for an interview dressed for a garden party or for bonfire night. But proper clothes (chef's whites are practical and comfortable to wear for anyone working in a kitchen) must be insisted on. In such dress any cook or member of kitchen staff is presentable in any public area. They will look professional, and put off no one. Indeed customers will be impressed. Similarly your bar staff must look clean, neat and tidy because from the start you told them what was expected. And there is no reason why a cellarman, if you employ one from time to time or even regularly, cannot look decent in a proper overall or clean dungarees. I think we are a slovenly race, lacking pride in our appearance. I am not advocating everyone going round dressed up to the nines but I would emphasize that cleanliness and clothing appropriate to the tasks in hand should be the norm, not the exception. You owe it to yourself. You, I hope, are going to be a professional. Just make sure those you employ are professional too.

Training

And talking of professionalism just remember that 'staff training' is probably the most misapplied term in this whole business. You will have noticed countless small advertisements in local papers under the 'sits vac' heading for 'part-time bar staff – no experience necessary. Full training given.' All too often this means a hurried introduction to the till and how to operate it. Nothing else. A man or woman working behind your bar should be more knowledgeable about the drinks on sale than the customer. It is simply not good enough to put price labels on the obvious things and leave the rest to chance. All too often an appeal for 'casual' staff means employers taking on staff who have casual attitudes towards customers and what they wish to buy.

Take beer, for instance. I like to know what the strength of an unfamiliar beer is before I ask for some. This is perfectly natural; an OG (Original Gravity) of, say, 1032 will be a thin, possibly tasteless beer but nevertheless may be suitable for quenching thirst at lunchtime, especially if you are a driver. An OG 1044 beer, on the other hand, is far too strong for most people during the day and is best left for an evening drink when you certainly do not have a car with you. Some beers are very much stronger than 1044. The price a landlord charges for his beer is a reasonable guide – the stronger the beer the greater the cost – but few things irritate me more when I go into a pub than being met by the blank stare of a barman when I ask him what the strength of a particular beer is. I bet that such a man or woman behind the bar will not know whether the wines on sale are dry, sweet, rough, thin or of sound quality. I bet he or she will not know the alcoholic volume of the ciders on sale, or what, say, a 'gin and French' is. I have even been in bars and asked for a dash of angostura in my gin and tonic, to be met with complete incomprehension, even though a bottle was standing on the dispense area. It is once again a question of professionalism. Training should be what the word implies. Your bar staff must know everything they can about what they are selling, just as your waiting staff should know everything about the food they are serving.

But do not make the mistake of assuming that lack of interest, or stupidity, is the reason. In Britain, alas, it is very often the basic ignorance of their employer. That, an attitude of contempt towards customers who dare ask perfectly reasonable questions about the products they are buying.

If your casual staff enjoy working with you (please regard staff as working *with* you, not *for* you) and they are good at their job and look set to stay, I would ask that you at least help with their holiday money, even though, strictly speaking, you are not legally obliged to pay them when they are not there. Now none of we 'small' businesspeople – certainly not newcomers to the licensed trade – can afford to splash money around and I doubt whether you could afford to pay full wages when people are away, especially if you have to find someone else to stand in, but the very gesture of making some contribution to someone's holiday is one of those small, appreciated kindnesses. Very few of us resent praise or thanks and we respond to thoughtful appreciation of what we do. It is the thought that will count. I would also suggest that at Christmastime you should try to pay a small bonus, again by way of a thank you. A small bar of soap will not do as a gift, though a double wage, or even an outright £50, will work wonders.

Now I am not advocating such generosity towards staff who do not pull their weight. You cannot buy good work, whatever personnel managers and union leaders may believe. A 'bonus' is just what it says – a reward (even more pleasant if unexpected) for cheerful willingness. It should not become a right, to be expected by the lax and uncaring. It may be difficult, I realize, to pay, say, one barmaid or cleaner or cook and not another. You must try to be tactful. But I do not think this will arise. After all, you are not starting out as a Lord Forte with a vast staff. You will probably only have one, or at the most two, local people to help you out initially. If you have chosen well, you will have no problems.

Honesty
The other complaint about staff you will often hear is that they are untrustworthy. Now maybe we have been lucky,

but we have never suspected anyone who worked with us of being dishonest. What I do suspect, however, is that because we trusted people, because we were patently honest ourselves, with our customers and staff equally, it never occurred to anyone to try to fiddle us, or anyone else. The problem stems from what I call the 'locked fridge mentality'. Have you never come across this? You can always tell that a landlord, restaurateur or hotelier has a basic fear of thieving if he has locks on his refrigerators. No matter what the fridge may hold he cannot conceive of anyone in the world not wanting to take something out of it without his knowing. If you are like that then there is nothing I can do to help and, after all, what does it matter? I just find it curious that such people always seem to be the ones who complain about dishonesty in others. I sometimes wonder whether they are trying to compensate for a streak of dishonesty within themselves. But it does make life difficult for yourself and for everyone else.

Now I know that some people will say that I am advocating tills being left open, piles of money left lying about, steaks and smoked salmon, quails' eggs and caviare free to anyone who walks by. I am not. And I do realize that if you are running a very large business then some security is essential. But I am talking about a small pub with one or two helpers. And I am asking you to trust those people whom you yourself have engaged. I would also support you if, at the slightest sign of dishonesty in any of them (providing it was proven) you fired them on the spot. But just do not make work for yourself unnecessarily. Trust your staff, trust them to get on with their jobs, do not harry them. Their enjoyment of working with you, and the confidence you show in them will make life all the nicer for all of you.

Feeding Staff

If you employ staff over mealtimes – and it is almost certain you will – then some provision must be made for their own eating. Do not, as so many employers do, give them a scant half-hour and tell them they are limited to a bowl of soup and yesterday's bread roll. Nor do I mean they should have the choice of fillet steak or turbot. Just make decent provision for them. Some casual workers may prefer not to have lunch or an evening meal at your pub, but eat at home when they have more time or their family by them. Fine. But please remember to discuss such matters with your staff beforehand, when you take them on.

Who Takes Over When You Take a Break?
One of the reasons you should try to build up a small nucleus of reliable staff is for your own days off or for holidays. It is absolutely essential that you take time off – preferably a day a week (some country pubs even close for a whole day, and there is no reason why they should not). And you will certainly need at least two or three weeks' proper holiday every year. Good people about you will help to reassure you and anyone who takes over in your absence (say a member of your family) that they have the support of people who know their way around. But do make sure that even if a member of family is to take over they are suited to the business. Do not hazard your future by being haphazard about your stand-in.

In the absence of reliable family or friends you may well consider a 'bonded' manager. Such people are often retired publicans who will take over the running of a pub in the licensee's absence through holiday or illness. They are experienced and their 'bond' (a financial guarantee between them and their agency) ensures they are honest. But if you do go on holiday and get a bonded locum in your place, leave it all to him. Do not spend the entire time worrying. But tell your customers first. They will appreciate it, and also support your replacement as much as they can.

Finally I offer what I hope is the clincher to my argument about employing good, trustworthy staff. If you have the right people, who seem pleased to see customers on your behalf as well as their own, people who smile, who make your customers, regulars and strangers alike, feel welcome, who are decently turned out and knowledgeable about their work (because you have trained them well) and skilled, then your customers are going to thank you for it and keep on coming in through your doors. Nothing is more depressing for any regular customer to his 'local' than to find behind the bar an endless stream of changing faces. It is quite true there is such a thing as staff loyalty. If you get that right, you will also ensure customer loyalty too. And that means good money.

11   Managing the Money

Let us spend a little time on the subject of money. It is, I hope, why you are in business for yourself. There is nothing wrong with money, and certainly nothing wrong with profit. But both are difficult to come by and yet very easy to lose.

Now the way you run your business will make a considerable difference to the money you take, your turnover in other words. It is a very personal business, after all. A casual remark, an offhand greeting, can lose you a frightful amount. You are going to have to work extremely hard just to get customers and persuade them to keep on coming. Do not throw it all away by mismanaging the money side and neglecting the profit.

Actually, it is all pretty easy. Providing you stay calm, stick to a regular and disciplined routine and keep a few records, the profit will look after itself. But do just bear in mind that you are not an accountant or a banker – both of whom make their money from being clever with figures. You are in the business of public relations; without steadfast and determined pursuit of customers you will not even have a turnover to make a profit possible. Do not allow meticulous book-keeping to blind you to your real task which is that of being a very good landlord. So keep it simple, whatever the so-called financial experts tell you.

Paperwork
Much earlier in this book I mentioned the mountains of paper you will face. I am going to suggest that you try your hardest to hand all this over to someone who will take care of it for you. Your life will be a much happier one.

But if you do not find such a person, and even if you regard balancing columns of figures as stupendously exciting, still strive to keep the bookwork to a minimum. There are people who will advise you to keep dozens of ledgers, each frenziedly cross-referenced. If you have the time and inclination, go ahead. But I would urge you to stick to the basics.

Keeping Tabs on Your Turnover

Now, to make life easy you should want to know every day the money you took for drinks and the money you took on food, if you are catering. You start every day with a float in the till large enough to see you through and at the end of each day you count the takings after replacing the original float. You will soon get to know how big a float you will need in the till. In the appropriate columns of the cashbook you should enter that day's takings, or make a note of the figures and keep them in a special place (I always kept a small notebook in the till itself in which I recorded both the lunchtime and evening take) and enter them in the cashbook later when you have the time.

You should also enter all the money you have taken to the bank during the week, as well as outgoing payments in their appropriate columns. You may keep an invoice ledger into which you enter all bills as you receive them. Not everyone does this. A great many licensees keep a neat folder of invoices in dated order, removing each one as it is paid and recording the payment only once, in the cashbook. Do not part with any invoice. If there is no copy simply put the invoice number on the back of your cheque before posting it. Similarly, if at all possible always obtain receipts for anything you have bought during the week. If you have not been given a receipt, make one out yourself showing date, money spent, what it was on and the VAT. Keep all paid invoices, receipts and so on in a special file. If you decide to follow tradition you will total up all these columns of figures on a Sunday morning and compare them (or 'reconcile' them, as it is called) with the cash in hand. The columns showing the money you have taken can then be quickly compared with the petty expenditure and the money you have paid into the bank. There will be discrepancies but only if they are consistently large every week will you have to start an investigation; you are either muddle-headed and have the system wrong, or someone has their hand in the till. Never take money out of the till on the spur of the moment to pay the baker, say, or the window cleaner, without recording *immediately* on a slip of paper, which you put back into the till, the amount you have taken and the reason for so doing. Replace this slip as soon as possible with cash from your safe, otherwise, when you are busy, you will discover you have nothing but slips of paper in the till drawer and no cash. Enter these petty-cash payments as soon as you can into the cashbook. Failing that, keep them carefully until that Sunday morning.

Arrange to receive a bank statement every month. Reconcile this with your cashbook. Check that the money you have taken to the bank is correctly shown and that the cheques you have paid out to suppliers have been presented. It will help you chart the progress of your business. Those statements, together with the cashbook and the folder containing all your paid invoices, are all the proof that the VAT and tax inspectors will need to ascertain where the money has gone. If all are kept neatly and properly, your accountant will thank you and his fees will be lower because you have done much of his work. You will also run no risk with the VAT or tax people. So far, so good.

But just bear in mind one simple point. All this bookwork is not, actually, just to satisfy bureaucracy. It is to satisfy you. The keeping of books is essential to you – because it tells you how well (or badly) you are doing and forewarns you, not only of impending doom, but the very definite possibility of success.

Just as should be the case with the VAT, never get behind with your book-keeping. What is (to people like me anyway) a damn chore becomes a hideous nightmare if you let a backlog pile up. Hence the traditional Sunday morning routine.

For all this bookwork you will need a calculator. A very cheap one will suffice, but if those calculators which print out the figures on to a roll of paper get any cheaper I would advise one of those. I have never had one and regret it. But then I am not only a fool with figures but totally inept when it comes to using a calculator.

The Till
The other bit of machinery is the till itself. But please do not get one which is too complicated. You will be inundated with salesmen trying to persuade you into the most complex money-machinery imaginable. They will promise the earth – that their newest model even cooks the evening meal or answers the telephone and gives the order to the tele-sales people. Do not be bamboozled. If you are offered a till which is too complicated, or capable of carrying out tasks in which you have no interest, forget it.

Ideally, the simpler the better. You take some money, ring the takings up on the till, remove the change, put in the customer's money, shut the drawer. The next step maybe is to tell you what change to give, which means another key to press. After that, perhaps, a division between drinks and meals, which means more keys. And so it goes on. And as it does go on the greater the possibility of mistake and frustration or both. If you want to know what you took on meals surely you can tot up the copies of orders which went to the kitchen?

You either buy a till, or lease one. They are expensive. So much so that some businesses leave the money drawer open at night, with the float intact, so that if you do have a break-in the burglar will take the money and leave the till untouched.

Take a look at the tills available (assuming you have not 'bought' one with the property) and choose the simplest for your needs. You should also have a safe. If you do not 'inherit' one go to a specialist security suppliers – the sort of firm which sells all sorts of locks, bolts and so on and seek their advice. They often have second-hand safes – new ones are very costly. Keep your main record books, as well as money and so on, in the safe. It protects not just against thieves but against fire.

Stock-Taking

All this bookwork is all very well, I hear you say, but how do I find out whether I am making or losing money? Briefly, one of the easiest methods is by the regular stock-take.

Now a lot of people make a lot of fuss about what is quite a simple, and quick process. When I first went into the trade I was advised to carry it out once a month which after a time became every quarter. I was shown by a most eminent accountant, who was a local, regular customer of ours how to do it. (Actually that is not quite true – our youngest son Hamish, then aged thirteen, was shown how to do it as the system was considered too advanced for me to understand, owing to my inability with figures.) This accountant pooh-poohed all ideas that stock-taking should be accurate to the last drop of whisky in a bottle, that everything had to come off the shelves, that you had to close for such a process. He said a rough stock-take could tell you more than anything else what you actually needed to know.

To this end we produced a chart divided into sections for beers, wines, spirits, food and miscellaneous items, such as cylinders, cleaning materials and so on. I wrote into these sections, on a separate line, our main products and left two or three lines for 'extras' (like the Pimm's I mentioned earlier). Vertical lines allowed us space for quantities and values. Each sheet was for one month, with a final section showing totals. Having got the *pro forma* laid out satisfactorily we simply photocopied a number of sheets.

On the first day of each month we entered into the appropriate 'box' how many or how much of each item we had and its value – its costs to us, that is, not its sales value.

First column was 'untouched' stock. If we had two kils of Bass, say, one keg of Guinness, two of lager and so on, these were entered and valued. The cask beers which we were using were dipped (special rods are available from most breweries or pub supply merchants) and the kegs slightly 'slopped' so that we could guess how much each held. The same process continued with all the bottled beers, mixers, soft drinks and so on, not only in the cellar but on the bar shelves. Then it was the turn of the wines and on to the spirits, the value of the contents of the bottles on the optics being estimated. It actually sounds much more irksome than it was in reality. The final estimate was for food in our freezer.

The total values for each column for that first month could then be compared to the totals for ensuing months, or quarters. The figures showed some useful things.

They told us, perhaps more important than anything else, that we were not carrying too much 'dead' stock. This can be a problem. There is a tendency to over-order, especially at holiday times. This stock then builds up so that it represents a very considerable amount of money which is 'tied up' unnecessarily.

If, as an example, our total cash value of wines held in stock on the first day of February was £250 and in June it had risen to £450 then was it because we were over-ordering or because we were selling more and needed a bigger ready supply? The same questions must be asked of all the other items. Well, the profit margin is going to reveal all and this is why you have taken the trouble to stock-take in the first place. Take a look at a simple chart over the page. You merely substitute my example figures for your actual ones.

	£
Value at stock-take last month:	3,000
Value at stock-take this month:	3,250
Difference:	250
Total purchases for month:	4,500
Deduct above difference:	250
	4,250
Total sales income for month:	5,500
Deduct purchases less stock difference:	4,250
Gross profit:	1,250

$$\frac{\text{Gross profit}}{\text{Sales income}} \times 100 = \text{Profit margin}$$

$$\text{e.g.} \ \frac{1{,}250 \times 100}{5{,}500} = 22.7\%$$

(NB: Exclude VAT from ALL figures. Inclusion of VAT leads to a totally false reading.)

Now what does this tell you in practice? Quite simply your profit margin is too low. It should be at least thirty-five per cent, as I said earlier in this book. The sum also shows that you are carrying too much stock for the amount of trade you are doing. You are also ordering more than you should. If the figures do not improve next month (or by the end of the next quarter) you will be heading for certain trouble. Your turnover would have to be enormous to allow you a gross profit margin of only twenty-two per cent. The lessons are clear: in the first instance increase your prices. (I bet you that a pub crawl round your own locality would show you the truth about your under-charging.) In the second instance reduce the purchases for the month. And third, try to keep your stock figure more or less steady for months on end, with the obvious exceptions for Christmas or Easter, or local special occasions.

Of course, you may well think that the examples of figures I have given are ludicrous. But I have to tell you a great many pubs lurch from one bad set of figures to another without realizing either what is going to happen or knowing how to correct a trend in plenty of time. Now obviously there is an off-chance that there may be other reasons. Someone has their hand in the till or is not ringing up the correct amounts, or are treating friends to drinks, or are stealing bottles of expensive booze. You have a very high wastage factor (the mice have eaten the beer pipes, perhaps) or you keep the beer so badly you have to throw most of it away. Yes, yes, accountants and lawyers have heard all those excuses and even the simplest look at stock figures and cash books and till rolls will give the lie to them. So which would you honestly prefer? Doing no simple calculations until your business collapses without your knowing it was likely to happen and why? Or correcting the problems before they become serious by altering the way you are running your business?

You would be a fool if you adopted the first course. The second, and wiser course could well mean you may be on your way to pushing your profit margins to forty per cent or even more. Success does breed success, you know. The trick is to plan for it in advance and take the opportunity when it arises.

Cash Flow

Earlier in this book, in Chapter 4, we took a look at another tool which should help you in your business life, the cash-flow forecast. It was all pie-in-the-sky in those days but now that you have real figures, solidly backed by profit margins you may think it a good idea to update that first forecast. It will be interesting to see how near you are to your original prediction.

If there are large differences you may well have made a mistake in the original forecast by being too optimistic or even pessimistic. You will be able to see, maybe, that you spent much more on energy consumption, or wages, or on new equipment, than you had projected. You may be able to see a 'lean' patch coming up. On the other hand, you may discover that you have more money in hand than you expected, in which case it can be put to better use than hanging about in the bank untouched.

This update of the cash flow is, in any event, also going to be a useful tool whether you need to borrow money or not. Your bank manager will be interested in seeing proof that you are careful and professional in the management of your business, he will be glad to know whether it is doing well or, if badly, why – and because you have made the effort, he will listen all the more closely to your plans to correct a possibly dangerous trend. Try to see your manager regularly and establish a rapport with him. If he is unhelpful, condescending or uninterested, you have the wrong bank. Look elsewhere for a better bank or even a better branch manager of the same bank. These figures will also help your accountant not only by relieving him of some of his work, as your good book-keeping has, but also in establishing a good and proper relationship between you and your business and the inland revenue inspector.

But as I said before, you are running a pub. Do not let any sudden passion for tidy book-keeping get in the way of that. And two hours on one day every week should be more than enough once you have got the hang of a routine.

12 Business As Usual

Like the well-known iceberg syndrome, seven-eighths of life in a pub is unseen by the public. But it is this sheer bulk of work which keeps the whole spectacular edifice afloat. And the public, the customers, do not want to see or know about any of it. And quite right too. All they are interested in is the eighth part, the part which concerns them most: how the place looks; how they are made to feel welcome; how good their beer or other drinks are; whether the food is acceptable (if food is offered); and whether, once they have left, their general air of contentment stays in their mind long enough to make them want to come back.

The Day's Routine

Remember that your day starts early and finishes late. The day is made easier if a routine is followed. The day is made worse if nothing is planned, everything left to chance. Obvious enough. Unfortunately a great many landlords do not seem to realize this. If they start a day badly, it can only get worse. But you are not like that. You will get up at a reasonable time and you will have breakfast, I hope. You will probably not eat again until the afternoon.

The first concern is cleaning. I hope you have a good cleaner who starts on the public areas as early as possible. You should look after the cellar and the bottling-up from the cellar to the bar, having first cleared the empty-bottle skip from the bar itself, stacking the empties in the appropriate crates. Remember, brewery draymen only take away full crates of empties – they cannot give you credit notes for partially filled crates. Make sure all the empties are neatly set out for the draymen and that they have plenty of space to discharge their deliveries. Draymen, for the most part, will deliver and pick up without interference from you if you trust them. It will make your day easier if you do not have to spend time 'helping' them with their own tried and tested methods of working.

On a clipboard or a brewery list you should add those items you must order the next time the tele-sales people ring. When you have finished bottling up – making sure that new stock is placed behind the old so that everything is used in strict rotation – you should place the order list beside the telephone. Indeed you should work to ensure that everything possible has been done by the time you open your doors, whatever time that may be.

Your Pub's Public Face
Let's take a stroll around. Outside first. How does your pub sell itself to the world? Are there dust and old crisp packets swirling round the door, old glasses on their side on broken tables in the garden, along with upturned chairs and used paper napkins? Where are the empties? Are they by the door too, crates stacked high, casks and kegs piled on top of each other along with empty potato crisp boxes bursting open with rubbish, apart from the black plastic sacks with holes in them for the flies to get at the empty tins inside? Is there a smell of old beer and even older chip oil to welcome people when they park their car among the old newspapers and dog ends blowing about? Are last year's hanging baskets still hanging, brown and dead and rusted? Are the windows grubby, the paintwork peeling? Good, good. You have a sadly typical British pub. I can take you to dozens just like that around where I live. Some of them are tied houses too. Inside such places you will find a landlord who complains about lack of trade, lack of staff, lack of money and lack of anything and everything – apart from his own lack of intelligence and energy.

But let us suppose it is not like that at all – your pub positively smiles on the world and, on a dull day, people can see lights, not only inside but perhaps on the signboard and in the porch. No rubbish is on view and certainly no empties. And no unpleasant smells ... Then it means the landlord of that pub has been out and about long before his customers, making sure they will be welcome.

Open the door, go inside. Does it smell of polish, with perhaps a hint of delicious cooking somewhere? Are there fresh flowers about the bar instead of those awful plastic things, stuck pathetically into old bottles and placed on beer mats? Are the lights on in the various beer heads and display units? Is there ice already in the bucket, with lemon and orange slices ready for any customer who might want them? Are all the beers actually turned on, and have they all been tasted by the landlord and declared to be in perfect condition?

If all that is done then you, the landlord, are running a decent pub. All you need now is a cheerful 'Good-morning, sir [or madam]' and you have already got the customer to return, even though he has only just come in for the first time in his life.

Greeting Your Customers

Now a word about the use of 'sir' or 'madam'. I make no bones about this, everyone is sir or madam to me. There is nothing servile about it. Politeness and courtesy ensure custom. It makes for profits. Don't knock it. It also serves another, useful purpose. If you are bad at names, as I am, you can never make a mistake by avoiding them altogether until they are friends, and not just acquaintances. If, perhaps, someone comes in whom you are certain is called Fred and his name is, in fact, Bert you have set your own public relations cause back to square one if you utter the wrong name in the hope you are being welcoming. Better to use the word 'sir' and never make a mistake until you are certain about the customer. You see, psychologically, no one objects to being called sir or madam – from the highest and mightiest to the lowliest, from the Lord Marshal to the hedger and ditcher. But they do object if you get their own name wrong. And why not? I bet you do.

Now it so happened that we once ran an inn and restaurant for what is described even today as 'the carriage trade'. We made no bones about the sort of people we wanted to see coming through our doors. Our whole marketing effort was directed to that very concept. But what some people, dismissive of such distinction, forgot, or chose to ignore, was that to us the carriage trade embraced every decent, honest citizen whose presence and behaviour enhanced the comfortable ambience of our bar and dining areas, while contributing to the sense of well-being and enjoyment in the other customers. The dreaded British preoccupation with 'class' had nothing to do with it – we would simply not tolerate yobs. There are probably more yobs working in the City of London than there are living in a depressed Glasgow housing estate, but they exist in the country too and it is best if you seek to avoid being regarded as a pub which has only cricketers, say, or rugby players or even local servicemen if you are near a military establishment. Ensure that everyone is welcome, yes, but that everyone is expected to behave decently and not throw their weight around, to the detriment of the customers' comfort and your trade and reputation. So, the way you greet and treat your customers (or, even more important, the way your staff do) sets the seal not only on your pub, but on your day. And you can only greet your customers properly and confidently if you know that the rest of the iceberg is efficient and operational. You, in other words, are ready for anything and anyone.

Serving Food and Drink
Whether busy or slack, always try to be 'quick off the bar', as the saying goes. Take the order with all speed possible, making sure you have got it right. It will seem difficult at first but experience will soon come. If a gin and tonic is ordered ask politely if ice and lemon is required. If it is, put the ice and lemon in to the glass before the gin. Open the tonic and pour a small quantity into the glass, setting the bottle neatly beside it on the counter. Do not drown anyone's drink. If whisky is ordered ask again if ice is wanted and place both water jug and soda syphon (if that is your style of service) near the glass so that the customer can help himself if he wishes. But watch the soda. If it is new it will have a strong jet. You may be advised to help

the customer yourself. Use your judgement. For beers ask
if the customer wants a 'sleever' (straight) glass or one
with a handle. If a woman wants a beer she would
normally have a glass with a handle or with a stem. These
special stemmed beer glasses are quite attractive and you
should consider buying a box if you feel your trade would
warrant it. Tilt the glass slightly so that the beer runs
down the side of the inside of the glass, otherwise the
'head' will get too thick. If a glass is greasy there will be no
head. In Scotland you are not allowed to pour a drink into
any glass which has been used – customers get a new,
clean glass for every order. Hold the handle of the glass, or
in the case of sleevers hold the glass towards the bottom.
Do not put your thumb on to the rim of the glass, or, worst
of all, into the glass. In the case of drinks like Guinness
start pouring that first of all when you take the order,
letting it settle while you complete the rest. If it is very
lively you can suggest pleasantly that the customer takes a
drink and lets you have the glass back to fill. The law only
specifies minimum measures so you must make sure no
one is served less. But even if you serve a bit more than a
strict measure in the case of lively beers you will ensure
the customer is a satisfied customer.

Always *think ahead*. You might not be busy now but you
jolly well could be in ten minutes' time. There are no rules
with the public. They will flood in and flood out. Just stay
cool and cope.

Food service varies from pub to pub. We found in our
case that a simple duplicate 'waitress pad' was sufficient.
The order was written down at the bar and the copy sent
to the kitchen. Do not bother with pricing at that moment.
Get the order away, that is what the customer wants to
see. Nothing irritates me more than to see my lunch order
written down, then priced, then the money demanded
and the change given along with a round of drinks and
then, last of all, as though it were the least important part
of the whole transaction, someone making their leisurely
way to the kitchen, my order clutched in their hand.

It is the somewhat odd custom in British pubs to take
the money before serving the food. I have always assumed
that is because the food is so universally appalling that no

customer in his right mind would pay for it after he had tried to eat it. And if he had not paid for it in advance he would not eat it and complain. Maybe it is just me being cynical but it is a system I dislike and will not tolerate where I am a licensee. In truth it probably stems from the legal prohibition on allowing credit for drink – though it occurs to me it is a possibly moot point as to where 'credit' begins. The law does not actually say that money has to be handed over from one hand at the same instant as the drink is handed over to the other and, anyway, in this day and age more and more intelligently run pubs are adopting the 'pay-at-the-end' policy where drinks and food are involved, simply because a discerning public prefers it. Of course, some landlords will always stupidly assume that they'll lose money because people leave without paying. The locked-fridge syndrome again. They do not realize that all of continental Europe operates on such a system and that the British are still one of the most honest races in the world. I have always asked for payment after customers have eaten – and I include payment for rounds of drinks as well – and have only once been deliberately cheated (by a very upswept, superior 'county' lady with three grandchildren). As a matter of public relations nothing pleases a customer more than to be asked politely if he or she would like it all 'put on a bill for later'. Such a question implies a complete and welcoming trust in your customer. Their drinks are merely added to the top copy of the food order, along with orders for any subsequent puddings or cheese. When you have a spare moment you simply put in the costs, add up the bill and have it ready for presentation when required. Keep an eye open for people waiting to pay bills, just as you would for people waiting for drinks. Once again, 'fast off the counter' keeps customers happy.

To this end, and once your pub has got a good reputation, you may consider offering your customers a credit card facility. This is becoming more and more popular in very good pubs which offer decent food but I do not think it would be advisable in the case of drinks service alone – a credit card would probably be construed by magistrates as offering simple credit, which is against the law, as you know. Your bank will advise you about obtaining the necessary registration forms and so on but I advise you to stick to the most popular and common credit card companies like Access or Visa and not be lured by the publicity surrounding other credit companies which may well charge you rather more for their services than you wish.

In your kitchen, whatever you are doing in the way of food, you will make life easier if you bear in mind what the French call *mise en place* – the laying-out for final assembly/cooking everything you need for your menu. So, as I mentioned earlier, all your sandwich ingredients should be ready prepared in bowls, the butter softened and the bread or rolls cut. This system applies equally well to any other type of menu. Do not have to hunt around for a bit of lemon, a piece of parsley at the last moment. What you are going to need you must have ready.

As the morning session winds down you must ensure the kitchen is thoroughly cleaned and made ready for the evening, whether you are doing evening meals or not. There is your own (somewhat delayed) 'lunch' to consider or you may do what many landlords do and have a sandwich or bowl of soup, something like that, and make a 'high tea' as the main meal of the day. But do not leave it too late. You want to be fed and rested before the evening session, not wiping crumbs from your chin as you open the doors.

The evening is merely a repeat of the morning. Replenish your bar stock, attend to the beers, ensure that if a cask runs out the next one is not only ready tapped but the big spanner for the pipe nut is laid ready for you to 'change over'. I used to be very careful with my beers, as I hope you will be, and had a bucket of fresh clean water placed beside the new cask. When the old one ran out I would take the pipe off and put it into the bucket, while my wife or bar staff pulled the old beer through until the pump ran with clean water. Once the liquid was 'clear' I took the pipe out of the bucket, allowing the pump to draw the residue through until it was all emptied. Then I connected up to the new barrel and the beer was ready for serving after about half a pint had been drawn off. This sounds a lot more complicated and time-consuming than it actually was. Routine, again, ensured the delay was minimal but the beers were splendid. Remember, however, to stand the old cask up on its end, well away from the spillage, hammer home the spile and a new cork bung which replaces the tap. The tap, incidentally, needs only a few light raps either side to loosen it. Do not leave anything 'until later' – that is how all sorts of tasks get forgotten.

Busy Times, Quiet Times
Most pubs outside the centres of large towns obviously find weekends – Friday night, all Saturday and Sunday morning – the busiest days of the week. But an odd night or two during the week can also be pretty busy with a different sort of customer. We used to attract customers from night-school classes at a big college of further education in a local town on Wednesdays during the winter, a very welcome boost to our income. But you will still get the lovers sitting silently all alone with half a pint between them on winter nights while you desperately try to stop falling asleep. That is how life is and you are going to have to learn to live with it.

Oh, and when you do close – don't forget to turn off all the beers and CO_2 cylinders, loosen the connectors on the kegs and gently tap in the spiles on the cask ales unless you keep them under top pressure. Nor to forget, of course, clearing up all bottles and glasses (which must be washed up that night – not left until the morning), emptying and washing the ashtrays, putting the beer towels into the laundry basket and throwing away wet beermats. Then you can turn the lights off and go to bed. After all, tomorrow's an early start.

Where is Everybody
But suppose nothing happens and no one turns up? Then you will suffer dreadfully from what is called landlords' gloom. You will probably feel like leaping into your car and furiously touring all the other pubs in your area trying to find out if trade is as bad with them as it is with you. I wouldn't bother, if I were you. It will lead to terrible rage,

for you will certainly find one pub (frightful, in your opinion) which is packed full to overflowing – and with your regular customers. I am sorry, but that is life in the licensed trade. If you knew how to combat that, if you could determine when it would occur and why, then you would very quickly become a very rich person. Just accept that it does happen.

On a personal note, we used to get extremely busy on Wednesday lunchtimes. So much so that people who came to eat had to be turned away. There was no real, traceable reason why it should have been that particular day. Then, quite suddenly, what had been to us the success story of every week fell apart. We were empty. Where had they all gone – and why? About two weeks later, Thursday suddenly became the day. Rushed off our feet.

Now it so happened that some rather jolly (but very experienced) licensees from a village pub about five miles away came in one Thursday, introduced themselves, looked around and said 'so this is the place where our customers now go on a Thursday'. Apparently, Thursday had been *their* big day. We said it had only just happened and we also told them about the Wednesdays and how trade had fallen apart only recently. 'Oh,' they told us, 'Tuesday was out big day originally – where on earth do the buggers go on Tuesdays if not to you?' I tell the story only to reassure you. It will happen and it will be a shock and a puzzle, nonetheless.

13   *Expansion*

Right at the start of this book I urged you to 'begin as you mean to go on'. In other words, lay good and solid foundations upon which you can build profit and success. Sudden changes in direction and policy make for worried customers. I know it matters less in busy city environments but in smaller pubs in small communities there is a strong loyalty towards 'our' pub and any dramatic shifts are unsettling. Remember, to the average customer of the British pub any change is going to be seen as a change for the worse – whatever the selfsame customers might say and think after six months or so.

However, where now? You have a good income and a profit unlikely to be badly dented by shifts in national fiscal policy. You are a well-established member of the local community and even the most doubting bank manager sees you as a sound investment.

You can do one of two things. Stay as you are, rolling along nicely and comfortably, or expand your business. These two statements are true whether or not you are in a tied or free house.

There does not seem a lot of point in wasting your time and mine on advice about staying as you are. There is nothing wrong in that decision, the wish for a quiet life. A great many licensees opt for just that course. They have conquered the uncertainties and the struggles are behind them. What better than to sit back, take a little rest and enjoy the fruits of their labour?

Keeping the Tenancy Ticking Over
In the case of a tied house, and providing your brewery is not one of the vast chains for which a policy of aggressive

expansion and a ridiculously increasing profit is deemed necessary, your tenancy should remain safe because your own knowledge, experience and expertise will ensure an increase in trade and profit at least commensurate with inflation, if not well ahead. After all, trade in such a property is a finite thing and every brewery knows it. It is no good wishing trade to improve dramatically if the system by which it is earned remains the same – same bar size, same kitchen, same building and so on. Ah! But here is the 64 thousand dollar question – *must* it remain just like that?

Now I think it is fair to say, despite my somewhat unkind remarks about breweries throughout this book, that a good tenant is not someone who just produces more and more profits every year but who represents that brewery soundly, runs a well-appreciated pub and causes no problems to anyone. It is expensive for breweries to keep on putting new tenants into pubs, and many houses, especially the smaller ones, remain snugly profitable and unchanged for many, many years.

Expansion in the Tied-House Set-Up

But supposing you, the tenant, want to expand. What then? Well, back to square one. Approach your tied-house manager with a carefully thought-out plan, just as you did all those years ago when you first went into the trade. You will already know from your contacts with the local rep how the brewery might look upon such a plan. Indeed, I would hope that your relationship with him or her has allowed him some hand in its formulation.

The choices are many and varied, so I thought it better to give some examples from my own experience. A particular one may not suit your requirements but I hope it will make you think up a plan of your own.

In the first place all changes and improvements mean expansion of some sort. What people think of when they talk of expansion often means building on. Not all properties are suitable for this. There may be objections from the local planning authority or there may simply be no room, as is often the case in town pubs. Conversion of existing buildings, say a garage, a skittle alley or an old barn or outbuilding is fine, providing you have such things. New building in something like a car park may be permitted if the car park is very large but if you are to expand the business by making the car park smaller the local planners will not like that at all. There are all sorts of snags. Hence the need for careful forethought.

But there may be one way round it which will be of great benefit to you as well as to the brewery.

You may remember that one of the disadvantages of being the tenant in a tied house is that when you come to leave you have no really substantial investment to sell on. On the other hand you are now earning good money of your own and you may care to think in terms of investing that money in a property – somewhere to live, a roof of your very own. In fact that is the one thing which a great many successful landlords do. But in so doing there is often a knock-on effect. If you move out to your own house, what are going to do with the empty rooms you used to use? There, in a nutshell, may well be the actual space for expansion.

Such expansion can take a number of forms. You may find that you now have a small conference or meeting room which will be private enough for local businesses or clubs for bridge and so on. You may be able to increase your bar size or dining-area size or improve your kitchen so that you can do more meals. And lastly, although, very much a source of useful profit, your own sleeping quarters may well be turned into comfortable letting bedrooms. You may even have room for a member of staff to 'live in'.

Now all these ideas will have to be discussed in the greatest detail with the brewery. Some will undoubtedly dismiss it (though few will object to your buying your own property locally, providing they are certain their own premises will continue to operate as a successful pub). What is on your side, however, is the very thing which I complained about earlier in this book – the natural greed of any company boardroom to make more money. So if your plans are going to mean not only an increase in sales of liquor, thus more profit for the brewery, but also an undoubted increase in the rental they can charge for the premises – and quite fairly, I may add – you are, after all, using their property to increase your own profits and they will want their cut too – then, put like that, it is an offer they may find difficult to refuse.

However, I should warn you that no brewery (or any other ground landlord if your pub is, say, leasehold) is going to fork out all the money for expansion/conversion. You will be expected to dig fairly deep into your own pocket as well. On the other hand you will be reaping a considerable amount of the extra profit, and because you have established yourself as a good business investment, you should have no reason to worry about being able to put together, with the help of your bank manager, accountant and solicitor, a satisfactory financial package of benefit to you, the brewery and your customers.

A Restaurant with a Bar?

You may remember, if you cast your mind back to Chapter 7 which dealt with food, that I urged caution when it came to this whole subject. But suppose that you had decided to provide something to eat and that your customers' approval has led to increased profit – and not only from wet sales? How to make capital out of that?

Well, it must be a very carefully thought-out decision and one to which a great deal of self-questioning, research, money and care must be committed. It applies equally whether you are a tenant or licensee of a free house, although the brewery will obviously be more involved if they own the property.

So far you have operated merely as a pub which 'does something to eat'. You may now wish to consider crossing the line by which you become a restaurant with a bar. If, later, you have spare rooms for overnight guests you will then have become a true innkeeper.

But, you may say, what is the difference between a pub which does food and a restaurant which has a bar? Surely it is simply one of words? Wrong. The whole approach will have to be different. People who come to eat in 'restaurant' surroundings do not actually want to be irritated by groups of beer- or lager-swilling hearties gathered round a bar close by. Going out for meal is not like that at all. And to be fair, those selfsame hearties do not want to have their bibulousness interrupted by waiters or waitresses constantly pushing by them with plates of steak and chips, if that is to be your market, or something a little more esoteric if you are moving up the scale. Both groups will feel awkward. Both groups will become dissatisfied. Both groups will start to look elsewhere. I said the decision will require self-questioning. I also said it will need research. Is there a need in your area for the sort of food operation you envisage? Have you truly spotted a niche for yourself?

I referred to steak and chips just now. OK, fine, if you are in a very large catchment area with very few congenial steak and chip operators. Such a possibility strikes me as highly questionable, if not downright impossible. Surely, by now, there must be no well-populated part of the country which does not have more than its fair share of steak-houses – call them Berni, Beefeater or what you will. If you are going to become a steak and chips place then you may be wise to remain just a pub – albeit a congenial pub which specializes in steak and chips for customers. Do not throw away an asset just because you have become accustomed to it. Your trading or sales 'gimmick' might well be that you *are* a pub primarily – something which would no longer be claimed by chains like Berni Inn, although many of those premises were actually pubs years back.

I hope I have demonstrated what I mean. Changing from a simple pub into a restaurant with a bar or bars can well be an irreversible move. You can build on customer allegiance by turning slowly from a simple pub into a restaurant operation because you will have already attracted many customers to you by virtue of your food and the reputation it has gained. And many drinkers will have become food customers as well, and probably amenable to what you are proposing. But the other way about is very different. You will be a restaurant which failed and getting drinkers back in will prove to be either impossible or a long uphill struggle. And you will never recoup that other ingredient I mentioned earlier. Money.

In Chapter 7 I said that food hygiene regulations are now becoming more stringent. It may well be that if you are a humble pub doing such simple food as bread and cheese, sandwiches and the like the Environmental Health Officer will not worry you too much, providing your kitchen is spotlessly clean and it is fairly obvious that you are a clean and responsible person yourself. But the scene changes, as I tried to describe, once you start into what may be called 'food proper'. The EHO may be reasonable with his timescale by which certain objectives must be achieved: but however fair it is you are still going to end up spending an awful lot of money. Far more money than you bargained for.

Now are you beginning to see why I urged such caution about serving food and why the 1990 *Caterer and Hotelkeeper* report that many pubs failed to make a penny profit from their food operation was such a timely warning? The crossing of the line from pub to primary restaurant means that your prime source of income will no longer be wet sales but food – and the serving of food will require both considerable capital investment in terms of kitchen and dining-room equipment and furnishings as well as greater expenditure on wages and increased problems with staff.

One very successful country pub I know, which began to make more and more money from its food operation – simply because the food was excellent and carefully designed to appeal to one particular type of customer not catered for in that area by any other outlet – decided to build on a whole new restaurant block. The decision cost a lot of money, as new kitchens had to be added. Unfortunately, in the opinion of many customers (myself included), the scheme seemed to lack warmth and vitality, both architecturally and from the point of view of interior design. It seemed to have been divorced from the comfortable, yet rather higgledy-piggledy layout of the original dining and bar areas, which had grown up naturally and cosily over a period of years. Customers were unwilling to go into what was a severely formal dining-room, preferring to eat as they always had done in all sorts of rooms grouped off the main bar, sitting on chairs at tables collected over many years from antique shops and old, local families. Those areas had atmosphere.

The new dining-room did not. Somehow the place never seemed to regain its vitality and although at the time of writing one cannot say whether success will eventually return, it will certainly take a great many more years than the landlord had planned to recoup the huge outlay.

So did he take enough care over the project? Well, he had proved to everyone he was an excellent businessman, a talented chef and an agreeable licensee but, I suggest, he had perhaps not taken as much care as he should have done in analysing the actual, specific *reasons* for his undoubted success up to that point of drastic expansion. What 'made' the whole place had been a judicious mixture, a slow bending over many years of drinking and eating. No customer, old or new, would have been able to point critically to any change, for change had come about naturally and stealthily – the adding of another table here, the opening-up of another alcove or small room in the old building there. The food too had changed. The ploughman had long plodded his weary way off the menu, quickly followed by chips and the attendant smelly chip fryer. Fish became more and more a feature, along with game and excellent dishes which owed nothing to, and had certainly never seen, any wholesalers' refrigerated lorry. In fact, for good or ill, this 'local' pub had merely reflected in its own slow evolution the changes happening in the village it served. That village had become the centre of a considerable rural area increasingly occupied by the wealthy or comfortably-off retired. It had, in turn, gradually lost its original population, that same population which had originally ensured the pub's survival as not much more than an ale-house. Had the pub not changed it would not only have lost, perforce, its old customers, most of whom moved to towns or housing developments in other places more convenient to those towns, but it would not have attracted the newcomers. Thus stability had been maintained, even though change was apparent all about. By contrast, however, it would seem that the building of a new restaurant and kitchen block was seen as a definite, *abrupt* change. It had nothing about it of the old evolutionary quality which had provided for an increasing local need over a great many years, as well as an increasingly good living for the landlord.

This abruptness apparently worried many people. Just why can only be a guess but I reckon I am pretty near the mark. Therefore, take great care about any change, especially in crossing the line between being simply a pub which does food to a licensed restaurant with a bar.

Another type of expansion is more suited to the licensee who is a businessperson first and foremost – and that is to take on another licence. This is by no means as rare as it may seem, and licensing justices see nothing odd in it, providing they are assured all the premises will be correctly run and supervised. Very successful licensees with ideas to improve other pubs owned by the same brewery are often more than welcome and there are cases in which one man holds the licences of a number of thriving outlets, though very much of the bigger variety in dense catchment areas. If you are such a person, however, I doubt somehow that you would be reading this book. There is nothing you can learn from me.

Off-Licence Potential

Give some thought to your off-licence potential: you are open during hours other shops are shut. Some landlords go into the off-licence business in a big way, selling sweets and chocolates, ranges of soft drinks and even cakes. There may be some call for this if you regard yourself as a village shop but I think most pubs should preserve a very definite image of what to sell and what not and should beware of treading on the toes of local retailers. I was once asked if I would consider setting up a local village post office in my pub. The idea was attractive, not least the salary offered by the Post Office itself. I declined because I reckoned we had enough work and problems as it was.

And while on the subject of off-licence sales, be careful about selling cigarettes and tobacco. Keeping a stock is enormously expensive and you may agree with most landlords that you allow a local vending machine operator to take over the concession. He installs the machine at his own expense and pays you a small commission every quarter from all sales. You need lock up no capital and do not have to worry about keeping it topped up. The vending company will estimate your needs and supply the correct-sized machine, calling every week to restock it. It is true that in some country areas you may be prepared to hold some tobacco or cigarette papers just for the locals who cannot get into town, but in most cases this is, in effect, a private arrangement. But having said all that there is a growing market for single cigars. We kept a box of good, medium-sized cigars behind the bar and were surprised at how quickly we got through them.

Expanding Your Free House

Actually owning more than one pub if you have a free house to start with is, I suppose, quite feasible though I am inclined to think it is comparatively rare. But free houses in the country or in rural towns can do very well by cashing in on the demand for letting rooms. In fact, the cost-effectiveness of letting rooms is very much greater than any other activity to do with the licensed trade. But once again, do some thorough research first. Have a word with your local tourist bureau to find out how many people there are actually looking for rooms in your area, and how many establishments offer bed and breakfast and what their occupation percentage rate is. Perhaps there is a demand only in summer, in which case will you make enough money to make it worth while? Perhaps there is a demand from businesspeople all the year round – you may be able to cash in on the sheer attractiveness of your pub. But be warned, appeals to the eye alone will not work. The way to keep customers is to provide every comfort and first-class food. You should be able to do this – the big hotel chains in Britain are now so expensive and often so bad when it comes to the provision of, say, a good breakfast that many men and women prefer smaller places. Whatever you do, though, visit local pubs in your area which do bed and breakfast and find out, tactfully, how well they do. Take a look at the hotels. Do they cover every facet of the potential market? And finally, will you need staff and if so, will you be able to get someone? As with all investments, do not rush into anything.

You will have to get permission, remember, for all

alterations or conversions from both the local authority and the magistrates. As plans will be involved you would do well to buy the services of an architectural draughtsman or an architect who specializes in, or at least knows about, the licensed trade. But do be warned: such people, in my opinion, often have quite frightful ideas of what pubs should look like. It has resulted in all pub interiors looking exactly the same wherever you go, complete with plastic beams, brassy gew-gaws and imitation flowers and plants. So make sure that if you do decide to carry out alterations they are not going to be too much of a shock to you or your customers. Tenants in tied houses are forced, poor people, to rely on the services of the brewery architect's department, normally with the most horrendous results.

As with tied houses, though, a brewery will often offer money on loan for you to complete improvements. Be careful of this. You will be 'tied' to a barrelage, as we mentioned earlier in this book, which may well become more of a burden than repaying a loan at normal bank interest. However honeyed the words of a brewery may be, never agree to accepting a loan without first consulting your accountant and then your solicitor. And it goes without saying that you should be on the sort of terms with your own bank manger to feel able to ask what he thinks about the whole thing.

Boosting Your Turnover

But expansion of any sort is all very well; what we are really talking about is increasing trade, your turnover, in other words. How on earth do you do that, with so much competition all round? Not very easily, is the glib answer. And slowly is the sensible answer. First and foremost, be careful. Gimmicks can backfire. For example take those huge, frightful plastic trees or play-houses, all garish colours, which you see in pub gardens. I would never bother stopping the car to go into such a place if all it could think of by way of 'attractions' was a hideous monstrosity outside it. Those sort of pubs normally advertise the fact that they have a 'children's room'. Ten-to-one it is a musty, grubby lean-to full of old crisp packets, bent drinking-straws and the odd shard of broken glass. If that sort of thing puts me off, then it will do the same for thousands of others. OK if that is the sort of custom you want to attract, if that is very definitely where your market is going to lie, but just think carefully beforehand, as I have said so many times before.

It Pays to Advertise

Now in that previous paragraph I mentioned the dreaded word 'advertising'. It is, alas, very often the first thought that enters most people's minds when they begin to think of increasing their trade, becoming better-known. Thus, their next thought turns to the local newspaper or 'freebie' broadsheet. Do not go any further. Stop and think a long while before you indulge in such an expensive, hit-or-miss adventure.

A quick look at any local paper will show you the deplorable state of advertising by local pubs. All of them say the same things, use the same clichés, the same old dreary promises like 'extensive menu', 'roaring log fires', 'mine hosts', 'traditional fayre', 'beer garden' and so on. And because they all say the same thing they are totally and completely ineffective. The money spent is wasted – money, moreover, that you could well have spent in other ways and more effectively: on an air-cleaning system, perhaps, to keep your bar clear of tobacco smoke – something, I might say, which is as much appreciated by smokers as by non-smokers – on better lighting inside or outside, on a coat of paint or new curtains. Advertising should come last on your list of expenditure.

For advertising to be cost-effective (and only ten per cent of any mail-shot publicity, remember, actually results in an enquiry) it needs to be well thought out, brutally to the point and brilliantly written. Just bear in mind that a great many clever men and women spend their lives writing advertising copy; they are extremely well paid for so doing. And they are well paid not because their employer is philanthropic but because what they are doing is extremely difficult. As simple as that. And you think you can compete?

For instance, I collect as a hobby advertisements from my own local paper which carry absolutely no address of the particular pub, hotel, restaurant or roadhouse in question. I know it sounds incredible, but it is true. Nary an address, nor even a phone number. The local paper either did not spot the mistake or did not bother to point it out to the advertiser – both of which are gross derelictions of duty. And that sort of oddity is commonplace. Hardly a month goes by without additions to my file.

Another common fault is the too complicated advertisement. Not far from my own house is a very plush country pub/hotel by the gates of a well-known National Trust attraction. Their advertisements tell you when they are open at lunchtimes, when they have candlelight, when they do dinners, when they do bar meals in the evening, when the bar is open in the evening and finally, when they do 'set teas'. The system is so enormously complex that I wonder how the licensees themselves even manage to remember it all.

Now do you think their prospective customers carefully cut out an advertisement like that and paste it on a wall, say, so that it can be consulted whenever they feel in need of going out? Like hell they do. I bet most are like me – they stay away because it is just too much hassle to work out when they are open or closed and for what. No, if the idea of advertising occurs to you, go away and lie down until it disappears. If, on the other hand, you really do have something special to attract the general public then spend a very long time writing it all out, then condensing it, then condensing it again, then thinking about it. Does it tell people what you want them to know? Does it tell them in such a way that they may be pleased at being told? Does it make them want to try what you are offering? And is it short, properly laid out so that it is easy to find ('catches the eye', in other words) and finally, is it worth the money it is going to cost? And take a look at it again: does it have your name and address and, if necessary, telephone number?

If the answer is no to any one or any part of those points, drop the whole idea. But if you have a good idea, and you get the advertising right, then make quite sure you can cope with the result. It can be dramatic.

Special Occasions

We once agreed to take an enthusiastic part in a special celebratory event in our village, a conservation area of great beauty, which was to last over a weekend. We did quite a lot of research and because the village was basically medieval we decided to try to copy the sort of food inns might have offered travellers in those days. A local baker who was knowledgeable about his trade's history agreed to bake some 'trenchers' – round, flat loaves of very coarse flour to be served with carved meats, local cheese and apples. Customers could have beer or cider. The all-in price included a contribution to village funds. We constructed the adverts carefully and laid them into the general village advertising campaign. The result was horrifying. We were packed out. We ran out of trenchers, meats, cheese, apples, very nearly all our beer and virtually all our rough cider during the first lunchtime, which was a Saturday. We still had Sunday, and the Monday Bank Holiday to go. Mercifully everyone turned to. The baker never turned a hair and luckily had plenty of the special flour he had ordered for us. The beer arrived as if by magic and some customers drove nearly fifty miles there and back to get more proper cider, cheese and fruit. What could have been a disaster became a triumph but it should serve as a word of warning to you. Are you sure you can cope if your idea *is* a winner? I know it is difficult to foresee but it certainly brings you up with a jolt, whether your scheme is a success or, alas, a failure as so many of them are.

But even in success, be warned. Do not have too many special events, mad offers, attractions of one sort or the other. Limit them. Use them as a way to increase your trade at other times. Word of mouth is still the most effective form of advertising, even if it is the slowest. As a personal example, yet again, we celebrated Burns Night, because of our Scottish connections, with platefuls of haggis, mashed potato and swede. The haggis was specially made for us and on one occasion the Fleet Air Arm offered to fly it down from Scotland because of postal delays. Some native-born Scots wore the kilt and the Highland Dancing was dramatic to behold. But what mattered was the number of locals and strangers who packed into the pub for a plateful of what, to them, was a very strange dish – and came back year after year. In November, near Guy Fawkes, we had a special 'banger' night during which we served about eight different varieties of specially made sausage, mountains of mash and quantities of baked beans. For a reasonable price you could eat as much as you wanted. Once again the event was a sell-out. But had we overdone it, dreamed up more and more just to cash in then we would have become less and less popular and the whole point would have been lost. Oddly enough, we never advertised publicly our two special nights. Just put a notice on our blackboard a few weeks ahead. The word seemed to have spread like wildfire.

Now those are only a few personal examples or ideas as to how to promote the attractions of your pub. I know one place where the licensee's wife is from the 'deep south' of the USA. Their pub has an Independence Day celebration each year, with special American dishes like Mississippi Mud Pie and so on, with a barbecue in the grounds or in one of their outbuildings if the weather is wet. It is very popular indeed, and deservedly so. But please spare a thought for the essential ingredients in all these examples: they were put on by people who knew what they were doing. The medieval lunches were the nearest we could get to what it must have been like and people joined in because of that. The haggis was of the very best and it was cooked and served properly. The sausages were not that tasteless, cash-and-carry frozen variety so beloved of all cheap caterers, but specially made. The potato was real mash, not from a tin. The barbecue and mud pie were really American, because an American ran it and made no concessions to what the English thought it should be, or the way they would do it themselves. You see, it really is a case of sticking to what you know and doing it very well.

Earlier in this book I told a story about selling Pimm's very successfully, cashing in on the hot weather. It was a neat example of marketing. There are dozens of ways you can market your own pub, wherever it is. Most pubs nowadays have guest beers. Despite the dreadful phrase it is still a facet of marketing – many pubs make a feature out of having a number of very good beers from other districts, breweries some distance away. Indeed, there are now specialized beer merchants who make good money from collecting beers from all over the country for selling on in their own locality. Under EEC regulations even tied houses are meant to be able to stock guest beers – a move at first resisted by the big, chain breweries and then accepted. It was an acceptance which demonstrated the real cynicism of such organizations: on the very day the new EEC directive took effect (in May 1990) hardly any tied house offered 'outsider' beers. The breweries had decided that if landlords exercised their EEC right then higher rents would have to be charged for the privilege. It was a neat trick. It also demonstrated the power, not to say the undesirability, of the whole UK tied house system.

Even so, marketing of some sort is still possible within any system, however restrictive. It could be a 'champagne' weekend in which bubbly is offered by the glass at a very reasonable, even knock-down price. In some areas like Southern England, and in the North around the bigger conurbations, it would act as a real 'draw' to get people to visit your pub to see what it is like. This is exactly what marketing is all about: getting people to visit you and attracting them to come back again. In the retail trade there is a ploy called the 'loss leader' – the selling of some speciality at very little or no profit just to tempt customers to come in and spend money on something else as well, or come back again in the future. There is no reason why you should not do the same. Just turn the idea over in your mind and see what you can think of.

The Future
Finally I think we should carefully consider the whole future of the British pub as we know it. I do not think it will exist, or can exist for very much longer in its present form. I would like to think that you are already planning for that sort of future and will be ready for it when it comes, or will even anticipate it.

For years pubs have had a 'shut-in' attitude, occasioned perhaps by the do-gooders who frown on drinking and people enjoying themselves in a way of which they do not approve. As a result the trade has become inward even so far as its architecture is concerned. How many pubs do you see with clear glass windows, where you can look inside at the customers, just as easily as they can look out? Still, alas, very rarely. I think all that is going to have to go, and the sooner the better in my opinion. Away with the frosted glass or the brown window paint, the heavy, forbidding door. I think pubs are going to be forced into becoming more open to the world and more like the cafés of Europe, where people of all ages are welcome, where you can meet spouses or lovers or (more importantly perhaps) where they can meet each other. And with this openness will come a greater tolerance, and, with any luck, less drunken hooliganism. It is this very sweeping under the carpet, this secrecy, that gives rise to reckless drinking by youngsters. In closed pubs, behind opaque glass, men (particularly) can feel safe from prying eyes and accusatory looks, safe to indulge a sinful habit. Remove the barriers and the pub becomes no more than a convivial place to go and have a drink, whether it be coffee, tea, alcohol or a lemonade, as in the rest of Europe – where, in clement weather, you can sit at a table on the pavement and watch the world go by. To this end we shall see decent chairs and tables, of a proper height, and not that monstrous arrangement you so often find in pubs where your food is served on a table much lower than the chair – an arrangement which ensures indigestion before you have had a single mouthful. We shall see the end of the bar stool, that instrument of exclusivity which ensures that no barman need ever serve any customer except those he chooses just because no stranger can ever get to the bar. We shall, I hope, see swift, courteous and knowledgeable table service from properly dressed staff whose duties also include ensuring every table is kept clean and not littered by old glasses and over-filled ashtrays. In short we shall see the grand sweeping-away of the detritus of old 'traditional' ideas about what the 'proper' pub should be – ideas which for the most part exist only in some advertising agent's mind trying to prolong the outworn myths of brewery chain boardrooms.

You, as a new landlord and landlady must face up to the reality that much of that cosy world is just money-spinning make-believe. For every welcoming, warm, comfortable, clean and agreeable pub you can show me I can show you in return a dozen places which should have closed down years ago and even now are only just clinging to their undeserved existence.

I do not think this is a very popular view to express but I do believe you would be very foolish to deny the glaring facts. I want the English pub to prosper, but it will not do so if the trade buries its collective head in the sands of time ... especially when those times probably never existed anyway.

So keep an eye on the future and be there when it occurs, not lagging behind. Remember, you are a professional and you are there to serve the public as well as you can. Which is more or less where I came in. I reckon you are going to enjoy it and I wish you the greatest luck your hard work can bring. I shall look forward to popping in for a pint – a tradition which is well worth keeping. Cheers!

Useful Addresses

The Brewers Society
42 Portman Square
London W1H 0BB
(071-486 4831)

Brewing Publications Ltd (as above)

The British Institute of Inn-Keeping
51/53 High Street
Camberley
Surrey GU15 3RG
(0276 684449 or, for the Secretary, 0276 686664) Membership is
through examination but the Institute publishes a list of
breweries and colleges of Further Education licensed to conduct
courses and administers examinations on its behalf.

Caterer and Hotelkeeper
Quadrant House
The Quadrant
Sutton
Surrey SM2 5AS
(081-661 3064)

Pub Caterer (as above)
Quadrant House
The Quadrant
Sutton
Surrey SM2 5AS
(081-661 3064)

The Hotel and Catering Industry Training Board
Unit 27
Park Royal Business Centre
23 Park Royal Road
North Acton London NW10 7LQ
(081-965 0066)

National Association of Licensed House Managers
9 Coombe Lane
London SW20
(081-947 3080)

The Morning Advertiser
13-27 Brunswick Place
London N1 6DX
(071-250 0220)

National Union of Licensed Victuallers
2 Downing Street
Farnham
Surrey GU9 7NX
(0252 714448)

Performing Rights Society Ltd
29 Berners Street
London W1A 4PP
(071-580 5544)

Publocums Ltd
New Chapter
Holywell
East Coker
Yeovil, Somerset
(0935 862560)

Society of Licensed Victuallers
Heatherley
London Road
Ascot
Berkshire SL5 8DR
(0344 884440)

Further Reading

The New Small Business Guide, Colin Barron (BBC Books, 1989)

Starting Your Own Business (Which? Books, 1988)

Starting and Running Your Own Business (Department of Employment, 1989.)

Index

Index